How to Make up your Mind About the Bomb

By the same author

Pricing and Employment in the Trade Cycle
The Measurement and Reform of Budgetary Policy (with T. S. Ward)

Robert Neild

HOW TO MAKE UP YOUR MIND ABOUT THE BOMB

ANDRE DEUTSCH

First published in 1981 by
Andre Deutsch Limited
105 Great Russell Street London WC1

Reproduced from copy supplied
printed and bound in Great Britain
by Billing and Sons Limited
Guildford, London, Oxford, Worcester

ISBN 0 233 97382 6

Contents

Preface

I would never have written this book if Wynne Godley and a group of friends, mostly from King's College, had not asked me in the early summer of 1980 to talk to them about British policy towards nuclear weapons. They caused me to think again about this subject and write a paper. It was when I found that they, as well as my family and various friends, found the paper useful and wanted to know more, that I was persuaded to go on and write this little book. I am grateful to them all for having made me pick up my pen.

Many people have helped me since then, too many for me to name. But I must particularly thank Harry Dean of ADIU, and Frank Barnaby and Owen Wilkes of SIPRI, for their generous help in providing information; Bernard Williams who organised a series of lectures and discussions at King's which I found most useful; Dr. Lawrence Freedman, Dr. John Inkson, Professor John Humphrey and Sir Martin Ryle for reading particular chapters and saving me from error; Mr. Duncan Campbell for permission to reproduce his map; and Mary Kaldor, Julian Perry Robinson, Terry Ward and Lord Zuckerman for reading the whole text and offering comments. None of them is responsible for errors that remain. Nor must it be supposed that they agree with all the views I express.

Finally I must thank my family who bore with me while I wrote this book, much of it during school holidays, and my secretary, Ruth Ripley-Duggan, for typing and looking after the drafts with great skill and patience.

Robert Neild
Cambridge, February 1981.

Introduction

Nuclear weapons threaten the lives of us all. Everyone owes it to himself and to his children to think about them and decide what policy towards them he believes to be right. Yet few people do so. One obstacle is a natural reluctance to think about such an unpleasant subject. Another is that the arguments and information presented to the public by both sides in the debate about nuclear arms are usually biassed and incomplete. The politics and character of the protagonists can be readily identified, but often not much more. There is no common framework of discussion within which the reasons why people take different sides can be coherently appraised. And much information is kept secret – or made hard to find.

The object of this book is to fill that gap – in so far as that is possible with public information. In doing so, I shall set out my own views, rather than conceal them. But my prime concern is to persuade people to think about the problem and arrive at their own conclusions.

There are three main questions at issue. Should Britain possess its own nuclear weapons? Should American nuclear weapons be based in Britain? What alternative policy might be followed?

In Part I, I identify the main considerations, factual and moral, which need to be weighed in answering these questions. Using that framework, I examine public statements of official British policy to see what is said or assumed about those considerations in support of the conclusion that Britain should have its own nuclear forces and have American bases here. I introduce my own evaluation and arrive at the conclusion that, starting from scratch, there would be no grounds now for Britain to acquire its own nuclear forces or admit American ones.

In Part II, I set out as briefly as I can the history of the nuclear arms race: the growth and magnitude of nuclear arsenals (in so far as it is publicly known); the possible effects if nuclear weapons were used; the political and technological forces and the strategies that generate the race; the diversion of disarmament efforts into measures which let the race proceed.

In Part III, I deal first with the history of Britain's increasingly peripheral role in the nuclear race, with particular attention to two questions of importance to policy: how far are Britain's nuclear forces independent of America? What control do we have over the American nuclear forces based in Britain? I then suggest what policy Britain might now adopt, given the fact that we do possess nuclear weapons and do have American bases on our soil.

Part One

Alternative Views in a Common Framework

1 The Framework

Assumptions
I shall start from the assumption that Britain neither possesses nuclear weapons nor admits American ones to its territory, and that otherwise the world is as it is – i.e. Britain belongs to NATO, there are American nuclear weapons on the Continent, and NATO's policies stay as they are.

We can then ask the question, 'Should Britain in these circumstances acquire nuclear weapons or admit American ones?' When we consider an alternative policy in Part III, we can ask whether the fact that we *already* possess them, and admit American ones, alters our conclusions.

The moral premise from which I start is not pacifism: I do not take the position that on principle I would surrender without a fight with any kind of weapon (conventional or nuclear) to any enemy. Rather, I am concerned with the question whether and in what way nuclear weapons in Britain make the prospects for us and our children better or worse than they would otherwise be. The economic cost of nuclear weapons is ignored at this stage. Whether it is worth paying the cost can be decided only when the advantages or disadvantages of having them have been assessed.

The Approach
As an approximation, we can say that we might find ourselves in any one of the following three conditions:

(i) *At peace*: no war and the values of our own society preserved.

(ii) *Occupied*: conventional war, surrender, occupation and alien values imposed.

(iii) *Hiroshima'd*: dead – or a survivor, or descendant of a survivor of a nuclear war, in so far as there were survivors.

The orthodox argument for nuclear weapons is that where a

1

nation, or group of nations, faces the risk of finding itself in condition (ii), the possession of nuclear weapons deters the enemy and so reduces that risk. But it may do so at the cost of introducing, or increasing, the risk of being in condition (iii). It may induce actual and potential enemies to acquire nuclear weapons they may use against you, or induce them to use those they already possess.

So to decide whether or not you favour having nuclear weapons you need to decide:

(i) How you value, relative one to another, the three conditions (being at peace, occupied, or Hiroshima'd).

(ii) What you think is the probability of being occupied or Hiroshima'd, as compared with being at peace, if you do not have nuclear weapons, assuming for the moment conventional forces to be fixed.

(iii) How far you think the possession of nuclear weapons reduces (or increases) the probability of occupation.

(iv) How far you think the possession of nuclear weapons increases (or reduces) the risk of being Hiroshima'd.

There are of course many qualifications to be made about the use of this or any other framework. The notion of time needs to be introduced as you think about alternative policies and outcomes: you need to think about alternative histories for your grandchildren. Moreover, in calculating what policy is best for Britain, you have to think about the indirect effects, if any, of British policy on the policies and fate of other countries, and the repercussions, if any, on Britain, i.e. whether we might land in some condition intermediate between being at peace and being occupied.

I shall proceed first by examining official policy, using this framework, i.e. asking what are the explicit or implicit assumptions on which policy has been based.

I shall then suggest an alternative appreciation of the variables and an alternative policy.

I leave aside a proposition which falls between pacifism and the type of calculus I propose to pursue here, namely that if nuclear weapons are now so numerous and so potent that their all-out use might end civilization, and if there is any risk of that happening, then we should renounce nuclear weapons

2

unilaterally, regardless of other considerations: we should not in any circumstances be a party to a policy which risks eliminating civilization. That is a respectable position. It requires an assessment of whether civilization is at risk, on which some information is offered in Part II.

2 Alternative Views

Present Policies

British policy is often enunciated in terms of making our contribution to the NATO alliance, the need for NATO to meet the Soviet threat to the West and other collective terminology, rather than in terms of a specifically British calculus. The standard position in terms of the variables defined above appears to be something like this.

1. Values

These are scarcely explicit. It is implicitly assumed that occupation would be horrible compared with peace. The extreme notion is 'Better Dead than Red'. There is little explicit contemplation of Soviet colonies in Eastern Europe in order to assess how nasty occupation would be.

The character and consequences of nuclear war are not discussed, displayed, brought home to people. Instead, they are underplayed in various ways: the military use anaesthetic language e.g. 'take out a city' instead of 'destroy a city'; it has been argued in the United States that she could win and survive a nuclear war; it is suggested that civil defence holds out hope of worthwhile survival, that it therefore increases our willingness to use nuclear weapons and hence increases Soviet respect for our nuclear forces.

2. The Threat

It is suggested that the Soviet Union and its allies in the Warsaw Pact are a united military and political force and that they are a threat to Western Europe: they might march across Western Europe if they were not deterred by military force. The 'threat' is mainly described in terms of the total strength of the Warsaw Pact's military forces rather than in terms of the political interests and intentions of the Soviet Union and its allies. But in an excursion into Soviet motives, the 1980 *Statement on the Defence Estimates*[1] says the Soviets are aggressive and appeals to 'Marxist-Leninist philosophy' to support this view; it cites Afghanistan as an example; and it concludes that 'Should NATO lower its guard or falter in its determination to defend itself, the opportunities might prove too tempting. As long therefore as the Soviet Union and its allies sustain and strengthen their large military forces with a pronounced offensive capability, we in the West must continue to ensure that our defences are such that the Warsaw Pact could never count on profiting from the use of military power.'[2] The section from which this is taken is reproduced as Appendix A. It is worth reading.

3. The Benefit of Nuclear Weapons

The allied strategy is described in the White Paper as follows: 'The strategy is intended to deter aggression, by NATO's possession of forces which are able to mount a robust conventional defence against attack, and by making clear NATO's ability and will to have recourse to nuclear weapons, should other means fail, to cause an aggressor to abandon his attack and withdraw'. The White Paper goes on to say that the former NATO strategy of massive retaliation was replaced by the flexible response, which 'does not commit us to respond in any pre-ordained way . . . . The step from one level of force to higher ones must not however be so severe that an enemy might suppose that the NATO countries would be unwilling to take it. NATO therefore needs a full range of options extending from a limited response with conventional forces through to a full-scale strategic nuclear strike.' The strategy depends on NATO 'having the necessary strength in each element in what is called the "triad" of conventional, theatre nuclear and strategic nuclear forces . . . .'[3]

The assumption is that if a balance of power in nuclear weapons is maintained between NATO and the Warsaw Pact (regardless of how large is the absolute number of weapons on both sides) the risk of invasion and occupation will be reduced or eliminated.

The justification offered for Britain's possession of independent nuclear forces and their renewal is that while the British

5

Government has faith in the United States nuclear commitment to Europe,

> ˉ. . . a Soviet leadership – perhaps much changed in character from today's, looking at the world in terms of values very different from those of the West and operating in turbulent internal or external circumstances – might believe that at some point in the development of conflict the determination of the United States could waver. The presence of enormous destructive power in independent European hands is an important insurance against such a misperception. The nuclear strength of Britain or France may seem modest by comparison with the superpower armouries, and so it is, but the damage it could inflict is in absolute terms immense. An adversary assessing the consequences of possible aggression in Europe would have to regard a NATO defence containing these powerful independent elements as *a harder one to predict,* and a more dangerous one to assail, than one in which nuclear retaliatory power rested in United States hands alone. To reduce now the West's degree of long-term insurance against Soviet miscalculations would be a most hazardous step.[4] [my italics]

The decision to base American cruise missiles in Britain is explained as a step to redress the balance in long-range land-based theatre nuclear forces, a policy which the Government 'warmly endorsed'. This category of nuclear weapons, in which the Soviets are in the lead, has only recently been isolated and treated as a separate category in which 'balance' is regarded as necessary.

4. The Danger of Nuclear Weapons

There seems to be no reference to the risks of possessing nuclear arms, i.e. the tacit assumption is that possession of nuclear weapons does not add to the risk of being Hiroshima'd, or does so negligibly.

The White Paper says that the Government believes that 'arms control can play an integral part in its efforts to ensure the nation's security.' But it makes clear that its prime object is not disarmament, that it seeks not to stop or get out of the arms race, but somehow to control the race without stopping it:

> Our aim is greater stability – where possible at lower levels of forces. Balanced, practical and verifiable arms control measures can serve this by limiting arms competition and making defence relationships *more predictable.** But experience shows that it is not realistic to pursue arms control from a position of growing inferiority. Our defence effort and our arms control policy are therefore complementary.[5] [my italics]

In spite of the arguments why Britain should have nuclear weapons, the Government thinks it would be dangerous if more nations were to acquire them: 'We believe that the proliferation of nuclear weapons would increase tensions, putting at risk international security and stability.'[6]

These official propositions scarcely seem to me to constitute a convincing case for acquiring nuclear weapons or inviting the Americans to establish bases *ab initio*. But they should be read for what they are, arguments to justify the next step in an arms race which has a momentum of its own, a race in which the risks taken in acquiring and deploying nuclear weapons may no longer bear any relationship to the political hostility or the intentions of the two sides.

An Alternative Perception
I now suggest an alternative analysis in terms of the same variables.

1. Values
We must be explicit and say how we reach judgements. Having visited the Soviet Union several times and most of the Soviet colonies in Eastern Europe more than once, at a time when I ran an international research institute in Stockholm, I rate Soviet

---

*Note that the suggestion here that predictability of defence is desirable contradicts the argument to which I have added italics three paragraphs earlier: that it is desirable to have a defence which is hard to predict.

occupation and colonization as horrible. It is easiest, though not necessarily correct, to assume that Britain, if occupied, would go through broadly the same experience as the Soviet colonies in Eastern Europe. In that event, the immediate aftermath of occupation, when a revolutionary government of native tyrants was put in power, would be particularly disagreeable for members of the bourgeoisie, of whom I am one. We would be unlikely to be killed, assuming we had survived the invasion and had not died resisting it or in some less heroic manner. Rather, we would be stripped of our jobs, status and possessions and put to work in a labour camp or in some humble position. Our 're-education' could be very nasty.

In the long-term, whatever job we achieved or became resigned to, the censorship, the lack of freedom to travel, the need always to be circumspect because party members and those linked to the secret police might inform on us – all these things would be oppressive; and so would the inefficient, bureaucratic conduct of the economy and social services, and the corruption that goes with it.

On the other hand, our children would be healthy and educated – though in some countries the children of the bourgeoisie have been discriminated against in access to higher education. They could find fulfilment if their talents lay in manual, scientific or technological activities or in sport and the performing arts. Indeed the encouragement of these activities must mitigate the frustration that the young feel as a result of the censorship of political and creative artistic activities, as well as explaining the strong performance of the Soviet countries in sport and music. There is always the possibility that with time more freedom would be achieved.

As for nuclear war, I have always rated it as utterly ghastly, though I realize that I, like most people, have kept the subject buried and so have formed secret perceptions weakly. Having now read and summarized, in Chapter 4, a lot of the standard literature on the effects of nuclear weapons, I have a more specific vision of the appalling suffering and devastation that would occur. Amongst what I have read, I cannot improve on the words of Earl Mountbatten of Burma, speaking not long before his death:

And when it is all over what will the world be like? Our fine great buildings, our homes will exist no more. The thousands of years it took to develop our civilisation will have been in vain. Our works of art will be lost. Radio, television, newspapers will disappear. There will be no means of transport. There will be no hospitals. No help can be expected for the few mutilated survivors in any town to be sent from a neighbouring town – there will be no neighbouring towns left, no neighbours, there will be no help, there will be no hope. [7]

2. The Threat

I do not believe that there is a significant military threat to continental Western Europe or Britain from the Soviet Union and its Warsaw Pact allies. Argument on this point is often confused because those who deny the existence of a Soviet threat most vocally are communists and their sympathizers.

The realistic interpretation of the situation seems to me to be this. The Soviet Union has developed a beastly political system through an unfortunate marriage of Tsarism and Marxism. And, having acquired a European empire in the aftermath of World War II, it is now an outdated imperial power, facing acute difficulties in holding down its colonies.

The reasons for those difficulties are two-fold. First, the message of national independence and self-determination has swept the world since the days of Woodrow Wilson, promoted not least by the Soviet Union in its youth. All other empires have gone.

Secondly, the Soviet Union brought a backward system to its European colonies, not a progressive one. The successful empires of the world, notably the Roman and British empires, brought not only technology which was beyond the dreams of the people they conquered but also the rule of law, peace and enhanced freedom for many individuals. The Soviet Union, on the contrary, brought an oppressive system to nations in Europe which before the war had established or tasted democracy. It was technologically and in many other ways more backward than they were. Thus, in trade, the Soviet Union has provided raw materials and imported manufactures (along with a developing exchange of manufactures), rather than the opposite.

Consider the history of Russia's relations with its colonies in Eastern Europe. Yugoslavia and Albania managed to break away from the empire completely. Half of Austria which was occupied by the Soviet army was released, and Finland was not appropriated, two developments which suggest a defensive rather than expansive military policy. In both Hungary and Czechoslovakia there have been major uprisings which were put down only by the use of Soviet troops and tanks in a manner which recalls the nineteenth-century treatment of colonial mutinies. In both East Germany and Poland there have also been revolts but these have been put down by native forces while the Soviet troops have sat in the background. Romania is in open defiance of the Soviet Union; she refused to join the invasion of Czechoslovakia. At the time of writing, the Polish workers are stirring for more freedom. Bulgaria is the only colony in the empire which has accepted its tutelage quietly.

There is no evidence that the colonies in Eastern Europe want to return to capitalism or 'join the West'. In the various uprisings, the main message to come through has been a demand for national independence, or, more specifically, a demand for freedom to make their own experiments with democratic and decentralized socialism, as indeed Yugoslavia has done. But Russia must fear that her colonies might 'join the West' and that the tide of independence, once released, might sweep across Eastern Europe and onwards into the Ukraine and the Soviet Union.

These are the problems of the Soviet Union on only one front. Think of her problems in other parts of the world.

She has bitter ideological conflict and military confrontation with China along a frontier thousands of miles long. Hence she must fear war on two fronts and feel surrounded.

She has lost the leadership of the communist parties outside her empire in an astonishing way, precisely because the invasions of Hungary and Czechoslovakia, and the manifest oppressiveness of her empire, have so frightened those who were or might be sympathetic to her.

In the Middle East, she faces a very turbulent set of neighbours and a Muslim revival movement that could infect part of her own population.

In order properly to assess whether there is a threat from any nation it is necessary to consider evidence of three kinds: evidence as to (a) its interests, (b) its intentions and (c) its capabilities.

(a) *Interests:* Has the Soviet Union any interest in trying to conquer West Germany, France or Britain and then trying to hold them down as colonies? I can think of no worse disaster for the Soviet Union than to be landed with more revolting colonies in Europe. On the contrary, she is an over-extended empire on the defensive.

It is sometimes argued that the Soviet Union may be aggressive in Europe precisely because she is on the defensive. There are three possible versions of this argument, none of which I find convincing.

First, there is the argument that to expand and eliminate your hostile neighbour is the best way to defend yourself against him. This implies that you can either occupy and pacify your neighbour or conduct a successful punitive excursion in which you spank him and retreat. History is full of episodes of both kinds. But I do not find either of them plausible *vis-à-vis* Europe now, with its highly organized, advanced societies and its military and political solidarity. As suggested above, to attempt to absorb West Germany and Western Europe as colonies would be likely to aggravate greatly the problem of colonial revolts, not diminish it. The notion of a punitive excursion seems fanciful, since it would mean war between the alliances.

Secondly, there is the theory that if the Soviet Union were falling apart internally, its leaders would go to war in order to restore unity in the face of the enemy. This is an old theory not specific to the Soviet Union. Whatever its validity has been elsewhere – which is debatable – it does not fit the Soviet Union. The main threat to the Soviet Union is revolt starting in its colonies in Eastern Europe, not revolt starting within its own boundaries. To become involved in a war with an external enemy is not a reliable way of rallying discontented colonies to your side. Rather it is a way of giving them an opportunity to revolt. An example is the 'Quit India' movement which erupted against Britain as the Japanese threatened India in the second World War.

Finally, there is the theory that in a row with China, the Soviet

Union might invade Western Europe in a pre-emptive strike in order to avoid war on two fronts. It is, however, hard to think of any more certain way for the Soviet Union to provoke war on two fronts, unnecessarily. For NATO would be most unlikely to attack the Warsaw Pact in the event of a Sino-Soviet conflict. And China, if she did contemplate attacking the Soviet Union, would surely do so while the Soviet Union was engaged in its pre-emptive strike in Europe.

(b) *Intentions*: Soviet intentions as expressed in the policy of détente, the Helsinki Agreement and subsequent behaviour, would appear to be:

(i) to avoid the risk of war on two fronts, east and west;
(ii) to gain recognition for the frontiers of her empire in Europe;
(iii) to ease the economic pressures on the people in the colonies, as well as the Soviet people, by normalizing relations with the West, trading with the West and so gaining technology;
(iv) to maintain sufficient forces to deter the threats they must perceive in the east and west, as well as to be able to intervene and put down colonial revolts when necessary;
(v) to promise 'human rights' so as to appease the appetite for freedom of the people within the empire and yet deny those rights wherever their fulfilment looks too dangerous;
(vi) to give military as well as economic help to 'liberation movements' and sympathetic regimes in those parts of the Third World, notably the Middle East and Africa, which are not within the United States' sphere of influence.

Thus the only area where the Soviet Union looks adventurous is in the Third World. All that need concern us here is whether her adventurism there would be a reason for Britain now to acquire its own nuclear weapons or admit American ones to British bases, had it not done so already.

This in turn depends on whether Soviet adventures are a sign of a more aggressive – or less defensive – policy towards Western Europe and so should cause us to revise our assessment of her intentions in Europe. The answer is surely no. Both superpowers spend their time intervening in unstable Third World countries

12

for the sake of hegemony, often perceived in terms of keeping the other superpower out rather than in terms of the positive benefits to the victim.

Both are likely to fail and suffer humiliations if they try direct military intervention in the Third World. Vietnam was an example and Afghanistan may be another. To people in the Third World, Russians and Americans look just as much like rich, white imperialists as did the British, French and other Europeans in the days of European empires.

The fact that the superpowers intervene in the Third World has very little to do with their intentions in Europe, where spheres of influence are clearly defined. It would have been a mistake for the Soviets to conclude that American conduct in the Vietnam War meant NATO was more likely to invade Eastern Europe – though they may have made that mistake. Similarly it would be wrong to jump to the conclusion that the Soviet invasion of Afghanistan indicates an increased threat to Western Europe. Indeed, it now seems to be widely accepted that the Soviet Union sent its army into Afghanistan reluctantly in order to defend and consolidate its southern frontier. An all-party committee of the House of Commons concluded:

> The Soviet Union did not go into Afghanistan earlier because the Afghan régimes prior to 1978 had been stable, even though not Marxist. Once a Communist régime had been established, the USSR had the double incentive of idealogical commitment to the maintenance of Communist gains, in line with the Brezhnev doctrine, plus the desire to restore stability on its borders. [8]

(c) *Capabilities*: If the interest and intentions of the Soviet Union in Europe are essentially defensive, why are their forces in Europe apparently so strong? The answers appear to be:

    (i) action-reaction in the arms race, i.e. the Soviet Union has been competing with the United States, which ran ahead in the 1960s, in a race which is subject to much inertia;

    (ii) that her troops in Europe are as much garrison troops as they are frontier troops, i.e. troops intended to hold down the colonies as distinct from troops intended to defend the frontier of the empire.

In so far as (ii) is the case, it is appropriate to deduct army divisions of her Warsaw Pact colonies from the army divisions of the Soviet Union, rather than adding them together, when calculating the potential military strength with which the Warsaw Pact might attack NATO. The troops of Yugoslavia and many other countries are relevant too. When this is done, one can easily draw up a balance of conventional forces which shows the Soviet Union to be out-numbered by the West. An example is given in the box on page 15. Nevertheless, the Soviet Union must justify its military forces in Eastern Europe on the grounds that they are there to defend the Warsaw Pact countries from a NATO threat. She cannot concede that they are partly there in order to hold down the colonies. She has to keep up the notion of a NATO threat to a group of united allies in the Warsaw Pact. And in doing so she plays into the hands of those in the West who draw up alarming balance sheets of the relative strength of the two alliances.

Of course, the situation in the Soviet Union is more complex than this. The Soviet Union is not now a personal dictatorship; its policies change, and so must the balance between different groups within the system, as it reacts to Western policies as well as to internal developments.[9] But to think about British defence policy it is necessary to start from a basic premise about the Soviet Union, a premise which will be qualified as analysis and discussion proceed, but which will be used as a shorthand in loose discussion and debate.

The conclusion I reach is that the right premise from which to start is that the Soviet Union is an old-fashioned imperial power on the defensive in Europe yet locked in the arms race. There are no grounds for getting excited about varying imbalances of overkill in different kinds of nuclear weapon; nor is the build-up of conventional forces in Europe, in so far as it really exists, surprising, given the scare which the Soviets had at the time of Czechoslovakia when their forces had to turn inwards.

3. The Benefit of Nuclear Weapons

I can visualize that for a limited period the advent of nuclear weapons and their possession by two angry antagonists may, by deterring both sides from attack, prevent war. But it is hard to

14

Alternative Extreme Calculations of the Balance of Forces in Europe.
The conventional calculations of the military balance *add* all the divisions (or tanks or aircraft) of the Soviet colonies to those of the Soviet Union and take the difference between that total and a total for NATO. They thus rest on the assumption that the colonies would with one accord join the Soviet Union in marching into Western Europe. It is implicitly assumed a) that no colony would abstain or withhold some or all of its forces, let alone that they would attack the Soviets from the rear; and b) that no Soviet forces need be held back as garrison troops to watch over and neutralize recalcitrant colonial forces. The only acknowledgement of any such problem is usually a caveat about the uncertain reliability of the forces of some of the colonies. A second feature of conventional calculations is that French forces are excluded. France, although she is still a party to the North Atlantic Treaty and has divisions in Germany, withholds her forces from NATO command, to which she would commit them in fulfilment of contingency plans only at her own discretion. These are extreme assumptions, alarmist from a Western point of view.

To illustrate the problem, one can make alternative extreme assumptions, alarmist from a Soviet point of view. Subtract all the colonial divisions (or tanks or aircraft) from the Soviet divisions on the assumption that a) all colonial forces would be withheld and would threaten or attack the Soviet rear; and b) one Soviet division is needed to neutralize one colonial division, just as it is assumed in drawing up the balance between East and West that one NATO division is needed to neutralize one Warsaw Pact division. Secondly, add France to the NATO forces on the grounds that she would throw her troops into the defence of Europe.

The results for ground forces (in division equivalents) available without mobilization in Northern and Central Europe are that the conventional (alarming-to-the-West) calculation shows a Warsaw pact superiority of 19 divisions; the alternative (alarming-to-the-Soviets) calculation shows a Western superiority of 36 divisions. Both figures are so extreme as to be nonsense, but one – the figure that is alarming to the West – and others like it, are bandied about every day as if they represented the true position. The truth lies somewhere in between. Details of the figures are as follows:

	Conventional Estimate	Alternative Extreme Estimate
A *Warsaw Pact*		
Soviet Union	26	26
Czechoslovakia	+ 6	– 6
East Germany	+ 6	– 6
Poland	+ 8	– 8
Total	46	6
B *NATO*		
NATO excluding France	27	27
France	–	15
Total	27	42
C *Balance*		
Warsaw Pact minus NATO	+19	–36

Source: data from *The Military Balance*, 1980-81, IISS., pp. 25, 110.

see how this can go on indefinitely in a world arms race in which nuclear weapons spread to more countries – unless those weapons are used from time to time. For, unless conflict ceased, the indefinite non-use of nuclear weapons would be indicative of reluctance to use them, and it would be likely to induce challenges either until nuclear weapons were seen to be unusable (because the user would suffer too much political damage) or until they were used: either way, deterrence would have failed.

It is conceivable that amongst some peoples nuclear weapons might become objects of awe, associated with a long-lasting taboo on war directly between their owners. But it is most unlikely that all nations would react that way: it would be a rash person who would advocate the dissemination of nuclear weapons to all nations in the hopes of achieving that effect.

In Britain's case, there is no unilateral or direct threat to the nation: there is no risk of a new armada.

Even if one thought the Soviet Union had aggressive designs against Western Europe, the notion that we need an independent deterrent seems implausible for two reasons:

(i) It is hard to believe the official argument that the Soviet Union might regard the United States as too feeble to risk using nuclear weapons in the defence of Europe and that, acting on that assumption, the Soviet Union would invade Western Europe, were it not for Britain's possession of nuclear weapons – weapons which, as noted in Chapter 8, are largely supplied by the United States and are independent of the United States only in a limited sense. If this argument were valid, one would expect our NATO allies in Europe to welcome our possession of independent weapons. So far as I can find, none has done so.[10]

(ii) I have heard it said by senior NATO officers and experts that once war started on the central front in Europe, no-one could stop United States nuclear weapons being let off by local commanders, a prediction which some strategists welcome since it reinforces deterrence.[11] That this prediction must be taken seriously is indicated by the concern which American military leaders express over the need to achieve better command and control systems for nuclear weapons and by the warnings of experienced military leaders and experts that in war events nearly always get out of control. Presumably the Soviet Union is aware of these risks.

As for the United States bases in the United Kingdom, they were established during the Berlin blockade in 1948, when bombers had quite a limited range and long-range missiles were years away. They were a revival of the disposition of forces of the Second World War. Since the advent of long-range missiles and bombers, the United States can hit the Soviet Union with thousands of weapons from its own soil or the oceans. Bases in Britain for American aircraft and missiles are not necessary. The continued existence of such bases in Britain can be seen partly as pure proliferation on the part of the Americans – more of everything wherever you can put it, and Britain is a very good aircraft carrier – and partly as a deployment pattern with political implications: the United States may hope, *via* the doctrine of flexible response, to confine a nuclear war to Europe; and Britain and other host nations in Europe may hope that American weapons here ensure American involvement in any war in Europe, i.e. they are a kind of hostage.

Hence American nuclear weapons in Europe can be reckoned to produce a positive benefit (we come later to the costs) only if it is assumed that the United States is a reluctant ally, i.e. if it is assumed that the United States does not enjoy its world role, does not perceive interests it must defend in Europe (as it does or has done in other parts of the world e.g. Latin America, the Middle East, Japan, Vietnam), does not have a military over-flowing with resources and in pursuit of outlets for them; that, on the contrary, it is reluctantly here at our persuasion, has alternative places where it could happily put its weapons or is eager to cut its weapons' programmes and military spending.

Since I reckon neither that the Soviet Union is aggressive nor that the United States is a reluctant ally, I find it hard to identify any benefit in having United States weapons here.

In addition to bases from which the Americans can launch nuclear weapons, there are, as we shall see in Chapter 8, many American bases and 'facilities' in Britain which are used for intelligence gathering, communications, command systems, storage of weapons and other purposes, the benefit of which to Britain – as distinct from the United States – is questionable.

17

If I were to put the risk of Soviet aggression in Europe higher than I do, I would go for a policy of improving Britain's conventional forces, not for a policy of acquiring nuclear weapons or letting in American bases, both of which are potentially suicidal methods of defence. It is not clear that this would require an increase in expenditure. In Britain the percentage of the gross national product spent on defence is higher than in any of the other European members of NATO, except Greece and Turkey. It is also much higher than in Sweden and Switzerland, two neutral countries with strong defences, and only slightly lower than the figure for Yugoslavia, another strong neutral. The reasons are that Britain spends a lot on developing and acquiring sophisticated weapons,[12] including nuclear weapons, and it relies very largely on highly-paid voluntary professional forces. Anti-tank missiles appear to be improving the efficiency of defence against tanks, though the extent of the change is still being debated.[13] There may therefore be scope for diverting resources into cheaper forms of defence. And if there were convincing evidence – which I don't think there is – that the threat of Soviet aggression in Europe was great, it might be possible to persuade the people to accept some system of compulsory military service – if the risks of continued reliance on nuclear weapons were made plain to them.

4. The Danger of Nuclear Weapons

In any nuclear conflict between the United States and Soviet Union, Britain runs the risk of being the victim of a pre-emptive strike or accident. That is what happens to aircraft carriers.

Probably the main risk now is that in a conflict outside Europe, for example the Middle East, the Americans might use, or threaten to use, nuclear weapons against the Soviet Union from British bases and so involve us in nuclear war. Indeed if the Soviets merely believed, wrongly or rightly, that the Americans were planning that course of action, they might undertake a pre-emptive strike against British bases.

This chain of events is not wholly fanciful. We do not have technical control (i.e. a safety catch or 'dual key' control) over United States nuclear weapons based in Britain, and the Soviets must know it. All we have is a political understanding, once affirmed in public by the United States nearly thirty years ago, that they would not use their bases in Britain without British consent (Chapter 8). During the Yom Kippur War the Americans put their nuclear forces all over the world, including Britain, on alert without any warning or consultation. Happily on that occasion nothing more happened.

This leads to two questions. Are the present and prospective leaders of the United States and Soviet Union to be trusted? And what degree of control do *they* really possess over the use of nuclear weapons? Shortening warning times, and the increasing sophistication of control systems and communications must reduce the power of the politician at the time of decision, compared with the military who do the pre-planning. In addition to that, there is the risk of the accidental firing of nuclear weapons through mechanical failures, human errors and impetuous decisions. There are known to have been many accidents involving nuclear weapons over the years.[14] That no weapon has yet gone off accidentally, or been fired at the other side accidentally, provides little reassurance for the future.

The Balance of Argument

To sum up, it is convenient to tabulate the arguments. The reader should check carefully where he or she agrees or disagrees with either view.

	Official View	Alternative View
1. Values		
(a) Occupation	Silence	Horrible
(b) Hiroshima'd	Silence	Absolute horror
2. The Threat		
Probability of occupation in absence of nuclear weapons	Substantial because Soviet Union is aggressive and can lead a united Warsaw Pact.	Negligible because Soviet Union is a latter-day imperial power on the defensive and busy holding down Warsaw Pact

	Official View	Alternative View
3. Value of Nuclear Weapons		
(a) In general	They deter and could be used in a controlled, limited way	They won't deter for ever without use; and you can't rely on use being limited.
(b) British independent weapons	Needed because Soviet Union is aggressive in Europe and may think United States is reluctant to use nuclear weapons	Don't believe Soviet Union is aggressive in Europe or that Soviets think United States is reluctant to use nuclear weapons
(c) United States weapons in Britain	Welcomed as a contribution to deterrence and as a United States commitment to Europe	Don't believe these weapons are needed to deter attack on UK/ Europe, or that United States is in Europe reluctantly
4 The Risk from Nuclear Weapons		
(a) British nuclear weapons in Britain	Silence	Slight, since risk of Soviet attack in Europe is slight; but there is a risk of accident.
(b) United States weapons in Britain	Silence	Significant. They might be used, or a pre-emptive strike made against them, in a superpower confrontation outside Europe, to which we were not a party and over which we had no control; and they add to the risk that Britain will be a victim of accidental use.

The first conclusion I draw is that if we did not possess our own nuclear weapons and had not admitted United States ones, there would be no case for acquiring them or admitting United States bases now.

Part Two

The Nuclear Arms Race

3 The Nuclear Arms Race: Magnitudes

Origins

During the Second World War the United States and Britain decided to produce the atomic bomb because they were afraid the Germans might produce one. The Soviet Union was not officially told of the existence of the bomb project during the war, though Soviet scientists had already begun a bomb project of their own before the German invasion of Russia, and the Soviets knew of the American and British project from spies. The United States used two atomic bombs against Japan ostensibly to save casualties.

The United States post-war plan for international control of atomic energy was rejected by the Russians – not surprisingly, since they would never have had a chance of acquiring atomic bombs while the Americans would have kept them for a long time. The Soviet Union exploded a bomb in August 1949, sooner than the West expected. The Cold War had by then begun.

In the first half of the 1950s the United States, followed closely by the Soviet Union, produced and tested a thermo-nuclear (hydrogen) weapon. Whereas there is a limit to the explosive power of fission weapons (atomic bombs), there is no theoretical limit to the power of thermo-nuclear weapons. The largest one so far exploded had a yield of 60 megatonnes and was let off by the Soviet Union in October 1961.[1]

The United States races ahead.

In retrospect, the Soviet Union appears, whether from economic necessity or choice, to have gone for small nuclear arsenals. But because of the Soviet Union's habitual secrecy, United States knowledge of Soviet arsenals was limited in the 1950s: there were no reconnaissance satellites until the early 1960s, and only limited flights over the Soviet Union by U2 reconnaissance

23

aircraft. These conditions, plus propaganda and pressure from the 'military-industrial complex' in the United States, produced two scares, the 'bomber gap', and the 'missile gap'. In these scares the United States ordered such huge numbers of bombers and then missiles that she gained vast superiority in numbers of these weapons. The history of the bomber and missile gaps is so important and extraordinary that it is worth recounting.

The bomber gap was in the mid-1950s. According to some American reports, this scare about alleged Soviet superiority in bombers occurred because the Soviet Union repeatedly flew the same bombers towards American defensive radars, round in a circle and in again, with the result that the United States gained an exaggerated impression of the number of Soviet bombers.

According to other Western stories, the bombers were flown repeatedly round and over a May Day Parade and that gave rise to the exaggerated Western estimate of their number. In fact, the scrap of evidence, true or false, on which the scare about bomber numbers was based, was probably not important compared with the predisposition at the height of the Cold War to see bogeys of this kind and the lack of open Soviet information with which to refute them. The result of the bomber gap was that the United States got 1,800 B-47 and 850 B-52 long-range bombers. Later it was finally estimated that the Soviet Union deployed only 120 Bison jet heavy bombers and 70 Bear turbo-prop bombers.[2]

The missile gap occurred after the Russians had achieved a technical break-through in 1957 by putting up Sputnik, the first rocket in orbit round the earth. Huge estimates of the future number of Soviet missiles were circulated and attacks were made on the Eisenhower government for neglecting the nation's defences. The degree of exaggeration in some of the estimates was astonishing.[3] In Table 1 the projection of inter-continental ballistic missile (ICBM) numbers published by Joseph Alsop, the columnist, who was the chief spokesman of the alarmists within the military establishment, is compared with the actual number of ICBMs as later acknowledged in the West – though some groups within the United States military rejected the high figures from the start. The table shows only ICBMs. The United States had a great superiority in some other types of nuclear weapons, notably bombers and tactical nuclear weapons; the Soviet Union was superior in medium-range ballistic missiles (MRBMs).

24

Table 1: *The Missile Gap: ICBMs*

	United States	Soviet Union	Balance (+ = United States superiority − = Soviet superiority)
		A. Missile Gap Projection	
1960	30	100	− 70
1961	70	500	− 430
1962	130	1000	− 870
1963	130	1500	−1370
1964	130	2000	−1870
		B. 'Actual' Figures	
1960	18	4	+ 14
1961	63	20	+ 43
1962	294	75	+ 219
1963	424	100	+ 324
1964	834	200	+ 634

Sources: Missile gap projection of J. Alsop from Ralph E. Lapp, *The Weapons Culture*, p. 32; 'actual' figures: 1960 and 1961 from Lawrence Freedman, *U.S. Intelligence and the Soviet Strategic Threat*, pp. 73, 100, and Lt. Gen. Daniel O. Graham, Former Director, United States Defense Intelligence Agency, *Air Force*, May, 1976, p. 35; later years from IISS *Military Balance* 1969/70.

In a post-mortem on the episode, Senator Symington, who had been Secretary of the Air Force from 1947 to 1951, stated that the high figure for Soviet missile strength was an intelligence estimate of the 'theoretical' Soviet capability and that by September 1961 the estimate of Soviet missile strength in mid-1961 had come down to 3.5 per cent of the original estimate made in December 1959.[4] He complained that on the basis of the wrong figures he and other American leaders were caused to believe that there was a missile gap.

The missile gap was harped upon by President Kennedy in his campaign for the Presidency. It is clear that by the time he assumed office, the gap had evaporated. Yet the political difficulty of admitting mistakes prevented a public correction of the facts or of the policies based on them.

Immediately after assuming office Mr McNamara caused a stir by saying at a briefing for the Press that there was no missile gap. On the following day, the President squashed this view, stating that no study of the subject had yet been concluded. Asked what he thought about press briefings of the kind at which Mr McNamara had made his statement, President Kennedy replied 'Well, they are hazardous in many cases – [laughter] – and I think our Mr McNamara might agree with that now.'[5] He promised then, and again a month later, that a new appraisal would be given when the review of the defence budget inherited from the outgoing administration had been completed.[6] When that review was sent to the Congress, no new appraisal was offered. All that was said on relative strength was 'It would not be appropriate at this time or in this message to either boast of our strength or dwell upon our needs and dangers.'[7]

It was in this message that the United States announced accelerated programmes for Minuteman and Polaris and an increase in the alert bomber force. These were the first in a series of decisions which soon led to the ordering of 1,000 Minuteman missiles and 41 Polaris submarines.

It was with reference to these decisions that Mr McNamara, after leaving the job of Secretary of Defense, argued, rather incompletely, that 'lack of accurate information' about the Soviet Union's future nuclear plans, combined with necessary 'conservatism', had caused the United States to build a larger nuclear arsenal than was needed.[8]

As they were developed, 'tactical' nuclear weapons were deployed in Europe from the early 1950s onwards by the United States. This term was coined in the United States, where the following classification, now in common use in the West, was developed:

Strategic Nuclear Weapons: inter-continental ballistic missiles (ICBMs), submarine-launched ballistic missiles (SLBMs) and long-range bombers with which the Soviet Union might strike the United States.

Tactical or, nowadays, *Theatre Nuclear Weapons:* all other nuclear weapons, comprising air-to-surface-missiles, surface-to-air missiles, short-range air-dropped bombs, short-range surface-to-surface missiles, air-breathing cruise missiles, artillery, depth charges, torpedoes, land mines and ocean mines.

This classification fits American eyes. It is not symmetrical: the Soviet Union may be hit by tactical nuclear weapons based on land in Europe, as well as by strategic weapons and by tactical weapons based on aircraft carriers, whereas the United States is not vulnerable to Soviet land-based tactical weapons – though it would have been had it not stopped the Soviet Union deploying short-range missiles in Cuba in 1962. Europeans may be hit by both tactical and strategic weapons.

The Soviet SS 20 missile and the American cruise missile, the actual and planned deployment of which is now causing excitement, are weapons which can reach from the Soviet Union into Western Europe and vice versa, and which have some degree of invulnerability through being moved around on motor vehicles. These, and other weapons of similar range, are sometimes nowadays called long-range theatre weapons, sometimes Euro-strategic weapons.

Tactical weapons

So far we have considered numbers of weapons meaning 'delivery vehicles' i.e. bombers or missiles which may carry one or more nuclear bombs, or 'warheads' as they are now commonly called. The figures for tactical weapons are in terms of warheads: they indicate how many warheads there are, including re-loads, for tactical aircraft, howitzers, ground-to-air missile launchers and so on.

By 1960, it is estimated that there were 2,500 United States tactical nuclear warheads in Europe; by the mid-1960s the figure was 7,000 warheads (excluding nuclear warheads in ships afloat and those for use by United States strategic bombers stationed in Europe). The figure of 7,000 is still universally used.[9] Though other estimates have been higher, the total number of United States tactical nuclear warheads was put at 22,000 in 1975, with the following location:[10]

Europe	7,000
Atlantic Fleet	1,000
Asia	1,700
Pacific Fleet	1,500
United States	10,800
	22,000

The Soviet Response

The Soviet Union must have decided around the beginning of the 1960s that she must match the huge United States procurement of nuclear weapons. In the category of strategic delivery vehicles, she had caught up with the United States in numbers of ICBMs by the end of the 1960s, and rather later she caught up in numbers of SLBMs. In both these types of delivery vehicle, she then went ahead of the United States, but she has stayed behind in numbers of long-range bombers. On this occasion the United intelligence services under-predicted the Soviet build-up of missiles (as distinct from warheads) – though not by anything approaching the margin by which they had made over-estimates at the time of the missile gap. With the benefit of reconnaissance satellites, *actual* numbers of Soviet strategic weapons have been visible to the United States authorities since the early 1960s.

Since in many cases they cannot be identified by aerial reconnaissance, Soviet tactical nuclear weapons are a subject about which relatively little is known, compared with Soviet strategic weapons, and about which demonstrably wild statements are made from time to time. Mr Schlesinger, the then Secretary of Defense of the United States, said in 1974 'our information on Soviet tactical nuclear weapons in Europe is not very good'[11] – a statement which there seems no reason to question today. For example, one major uncertainty is how far Warsaw Pact tactical aircraft are set to carry nuclear weapons in war, as distinct from having the theoretical capability to do so attributed to them by the military in the West. Given the uncertainty, it is hard to know what to make of the statement in the British Defence White Paper for 1980 (Para. 219) that the Warsaw Pact has a lead over NATO in numbers of both long-range and short-range 'theatre nuclear systems' i.e. delivery systems, not warheads. It is a statement which contradicts the traditional view that the Warsaw Pact enjoys superiority in numbers of conventional forces, and places less emphasis than NATO on the possession of battlefield nuclear weapons – though the Soviet Union did at a relatively early stage develop a substantial force of medium-range missiles. The whole White Paper, which sets out to justify the acquisition by Britain of a new generation of nuclear weapons, smacks of alarmism.

28

The Present State of Play

There are so many variables which determine the capacity of a given weapon to cause destruction, that it would not be possible to compare the relative nuclear strength of the Soviet Union and United States with precision even if information were complete. But we can look at the main variables for which there is information, and consider what is the combined capacity to inflict damage of the two forces, starting with strategic weapons. The principal variables that matter are:

(a) The number of *delivery vehicles* (ICBMs, SLBMs and long-range bombers) – though it is important to note that because of the remoteness of their bases, a far smaller proportion of Soviet submarines can be kept 'on station', within firing range of the United States, than is the case for United States submarines facing the Soviet Union.

(b) The number of *warheads* per delivery vehicle: a single bomber may carry several bombs or air-to-ground guided missiles; a single ballistic missile may carry several warheads which in the simplest version may fall in a fixed cluster (MRVs), in the present advanced version may be aimed independently at separate targets (MIRVs), and in the version that is now in the pipeline, may manoeuvre themselves on the way to their targets (MaRVs).

(c) The *yield* in kilotonnes or megatonnes (kt. or mt.) i.e. the energy released by a warhead measured in equivalent weight of TNT.

(d) The *accuracy* with which the warheads can be expected to hit the target. This is important, particularly where one is considering the probability of destroying a target by blast (rather than fire or radiation). For the relationship between the radius of destruction by blast of a nuclear weapon and its explosive yield (defined above) follows a cube law: making a weapon twice as accurate (i.e. halving the radius within which a given proportion of warheads can be expected to land) has the same effect as making the warhead eight (two cubed) times as powerful – or permits you to make the warhead one-eighth as powerful as

29

before and still have the same probability of destroying a point target by blast.[12]

(e) A further yardstick is *'throw-weight'*, the load that a missile or bomber can throw at the enemy. Its significance depends on how far big loads are needed to compensate for low accuracy, how far warheads have been miniaturized, and so on.

Estimates for the strategic weapons of the two superpowers in 1979 are given in Table 2.

Table 2: *Strategic Weapons of the Soviet Union and United States*

	Number of delivery vehicles (no.)	Throw-weight (millions of pounds)	Number of warheads (no.)	Megatonnage (approx) (mt.)
Soviet Union:	2,504	11.3	5,000	4,800
United States:[a]	2,064	7.2	9,200	3,200
Total:	4,568	18.5	14,200	8,000

a: Excluding 220 non-operational B.52 bombers.
Source: SIPRI Yearbook 1980, p.222 and pp. XXVII, XXVIII.

Under the Salt II agreements, which have not been ratified but are being informally observed, each superpower is meant to reduce the number of delivery vehicles to 2,250 over the next couple of years (the 220 non-operational B-52s being included for this purpose in the calculation of United States forces). But the number of delivery vehicles which, under Salt II, may be fitted with MIRVs (or, in the case of bombers, long-range cruise missiles) is such that it is estimated that, by 1985, each superpower may have something over 10,000 strategic warheads.[13] The demise of Salt II would be unlikely to make the figure less.

The next step is to add on as best we can figures for the tactical nuclear warheads of the two superpowers. For the United States, we can add on 22,000 as given earlier – though it should be remembered that other estimates run higher. For the Soviet

Union, a rough procedure is to assume that it has fewer warheads in Europe than the United States, plus some on the China front, say 5,000 altogether. The total for the tactical weapons is then 27,000.

The secondary nuclear powers – Britain, China and France – may add 2,000 or so to the world total of warheads. For example, Britain has 192 warheads in her four Polaris submarines, plus an unknown number in tactical delivery systems and 48 Vulcan bombers. France has a similar number of delivery systems, but it may have fewer warheads since it has yet to install multiple warheads in its missiles. China, with a small number of missiles and bombers, appears likely to have fewer warheads than France or Britain.

The megatonnage of the French nuclear force has been stated by the French Minister of Defence to have been 22 mt. in 1976 and to be going to exceed 80 mt. in 1982.[14] By interpolation, one can assume that it may now be around 50 mt. Britain's Polaris A3 missiles have a total of 38 mt. With other weapons the British total may be around 100 mt., at a guess.

If we try adding up all these figures to obtain world totals, we get a figure of about 50,000 for the total number of warheads, rising primarily because of the introduction of multiple warheads. Any figure for total megatonnage is much more hazardous, since tactical nuclear weapons are so various and obscure. But starting from the figure of about 8,000 mt. for the strategic weapons of the two superpowers and adding a rough allowance for their tactical weapons and for the weapons of the secondary nuclear powers, we are bound to reach a total above 10,000 mt., and could plausibly reach 15,000 mt. or more.

A similar estimate is to be found in the statement by Dr Sigvard Eklund, Director-General of the International Atomic Energy Agency, that 'There may now exist some 50,000 nuclear weapons, the combined explosive power of which is believed to be equal to that of more than one million Hiroshima bombs, or not less than three tons of TNT for every individual in the world.'[15] That implies a total yield of about 15,000 mt.

These figures are probably conservative. In 1960, Senator (later President) Kennedy spoke of ten tons per person on the globe, implying a total of 30,000 mt., and Professor York suggested 60,000 mt.[16] Since then the size of the average warhead has been reduced as accuracies have been improved, but the number of warheads has increased. All the totals are so enormous that the difference between them matters little.

4 The Effect of Nuclear Weapons

What would be the effect if one or more of these weapons were used?

It is a horrible subject to contemplate, but it is vitally important that we should all bring ourselves to look at the available evidence so that we know the nature of the risks that go with nuclear arms. The data consist of:

(i) evidence from Hiroshima and Nagasaki, the two places where nuclear weapons have so far been used in anger; and

(ii) evidence from tests of nuclear weapons, of which there have been 1,200 or more since 1945 (as we see in Chapter 7).

From these data it is possible to estimate with some confidence the effect of one weapon and to model, with limited confidence, the effects of an all-out nuclear exchange. A variety of exercises of both kinds has been conducted. As with most aspects of nuclear arms, far more has been published in the United States than elsewhere.

The effects of a single bomb

Eighty per cent or more of the energy from a nuclear explosion is released as a blast wave (which travels relatively slowly, though at first faster than the speed of sound) and a pulse of intense heat (which travels at the speed of light) and whose duration depends on the size of the bomb: 1 second for a 10 kt. explosion and 10 seconds for a 1 mt. explosion.

In order to indicate the effects of the blast and heat, Table 3, derived from a report by the United States Arms Control and Disarmament Agency (ACDA) shows what would happen at different distances, described by concentric circles, from an airburst explosion. The first circle is the innermost one. Here everything would be destroyed and most people killed outright. At the limits of this circle the blast would cause an overpressure of 20 pounds per square inch and the wind would reach 500 m.p.h. The radius of this circle is 1.5 miles for a 1 mt. weapon and 1.2 miles for a 500 kt. weapon. (The cube law, noted in Chapter 3, prevents the difference being great.)

Table 3: *Effects of an Airburst Weapon – 1 Megaton and 500 Kilotons*

	1st Circle	2nd Circle	3rd Circle	4th Circle	5th Circle	6th Circle
1. Conditions at the limit of the circle						
(a) Overpressure (pounds per square inch)	20	10	5	na	na	2
(b) Windspeed (miles per hour)	500	300	160	na	na	na
(c) Heat (calories per square centimetre)	na	na	na	25	12	~6
2. Effect	Reinforced concrete buildings destroyed	Concrete buildings destroyed	Brick and wood-frame houses destroyed	Spontaneous ignition of clothing and household combustibles	Third degree burns to all exposed skin	Moderate damage to brick and wood-frame houses; 50% chance of 2nd degree burns
3. Radius of the circle from point of explosion (statute miles) for						
(a) 1 megaton bomb	1.5	2.9	4.2	4.9	6.2	8.5
(b) 500 kiloton bomb	1.2	2.3	3.3	3.8	4.9	6.8

Source: The Effects of Nuclear War, U.S. Arms Control and Disarmament Agency, April 1979.
na: not available.

The limits of the next two circles are described by the intensity of blast, though there would also be intense heat. In the whole area encompassed by the limits of the third circle (radius 4.2 miles for 1 mt., 3.3 miles for 500 kt.) few people will survive who have not sought and found protection in strong structures or shelters which will withstand the fire, blast and shock and which will attenuate radiation.

Blast continues to be important beyond the limits of the fifth circle, whose radius is 6.2 miles for a 1 mt. weapon, 4.9 miles for 500 kt. This is because blast even as weak as two pounds to the square inch or so first compresses the walls out of houses, which does relatively little damage, but then sucks the walls out, causing the roof and floors to crash downwards onto those inside, and causing roads to be blocked by rubble.

Fire too continues for great distances, though buildings will shield one another and will shield persons in their shadow. The spontaneous combustion of clothing and combustible household materials (curtains, furniture etc.) will occur to the limits of the fourth circle; third degree burns to all exposed skin to the limits of the fifth circle; and a 50 per cent chance of second degree burns to exposed skin to the limits of the sixth circle (radius 8.5 – 6.8 miles).

The definition of second and third degree burns is:

Second degree burns: 'In second degree burns the skin is blistered and the blisters may break. The upper and intermediate skin cells are killed but the deepest cells of the skin are not; the skin is usually reddened, swollen and if the blisters are broken, weeping. Will heal in 6 weeks or less with slight scarring.'

Third degree burns: 'The full thickness of the skin and more or less underlying tissue is destroyed. The area looks dead white, brown, bright red or charred, and may not be swollen at first. . . . Burns more than 2in. in diameter will heal only after months of treatment and with great scarring and deformity unless early grafting operations are done.'[1]

If more than 10 to 30 per cent of the surface area of the body is burnt, the victim is likely, in the absence of special hospital care, to die from shock even in the case of second-degree burns.

Apart from burns and blast, people may be temporarily blinded by the flash of a nuclear explosion. According to a recent report to the Assembly of the Western European Union (WEU),

'. . . if the eye happens to be looking at the fireball at the time of the explosion permanent blindness can result at distances up to 60 kilometres' (nearly 40 miles).[2]

There will also be the two forms of damage from nuclear radiation; direct radiation emitted at the time of the explosion, and fallout radiation from material swept up from the ground and rendered radioactive by the explosion.

For a bomb of given explosive power both direct radiation and fallout will vary according to the design of the bomb. For example, the neutron bomb, which both the United States and France have considered deploying for battlefield use in Europe, would produce a lot of nuclear radiation, which damages people only, in relation to blast and thermal radiation.

Broadly speaking, it appears that for a typical weapon (i.e. above about 20 kt.) in normal conditions direct radiation will be concentrated within the area where many people will be killed or maimed by blast and fire anyway. So it may not greatly add to numbers initially killed and injured – though it will compound injuries and so increase delayed deaths.

Fallout, on the other hand, both extends the area affected by a bomb and prolongs the period in which injury is suffered. It can be divided into two categories – *early fallout* consisting of radioactive particles reaching the ground within 24 hours of an explosion, and *delayed fallout,* consisting of particles carried high into the atmosphere which will fall back to earth for a period of up to several years.

Significant early fallout will not occur with an 'airburst', i.e. if a weapon is exploded high enough for the fireball not to reach the ground and produce radioactive dust from the soil and debris, but it will occur with a 'groundburst'. Since groundbursts are the way to destroy silos containing missiles and to deal with other hardened targets, they are increasingly likely as the Soviet Union and United States adopt the strategy of aiming at each other's weapons. For the rest, the amount of early fallout will vary greatly with the nature of the ground, the wind and the rain, as well as with the design of the bomb: bombs can be 'salted' or made 'dirty' so as to produce increased fallout.

A groundburst will produce early fallout in a cigar-shaped area extending downwind. As you go further from the point of explosion, the interval before the fallout arrives will increase and the amount of fallout will diminish.

According to the WEU report, 'Typically, fallout from a single 1 megaton groundburst with 25 kph wind can be expected to produce 20% deaths in unprotected persons in an area 20 km wide extending to 100 km downwind from the point of explosion, clinical effects would be observable (dose of 100 rads) in persons exposed up to 200 km downwind, and radiation from fallout would be measurable over more than twice that distance. The dose rate would reach a maximum in one hour to one day, depending on distance from the explosion, and would decline thereafter due to radioactive decay, falling to one-thousandth of the initial maximum in two weeks, by which time the dose received by an exposed person would be 90% of the dose to be expected from a permanent stay at the same spot.'[3] The report goes on to explain that this is why two weeks is a rule of thumb period during which civilian populations would be expected to stay in fallout shelters. Although shielding will be more effective than it is against initial nuclear radiation emitted in the vicinity of an explosion (because the energies are less), radiation from fallout is emitted invisibly from all surfaces contaminated by fallout, including the roofs of buildings and the skin and clothing of exposed persons.

Further direct effects of a nuclear explosion include two associated with bursts at high altitude:

(a) The generation of an electro-magnetic pulse (EMP) which can damage electrical and, in particular, electronic equipment, if the equipment is not protected. The WEU Report tells us that 'It is now believed that a single nuclear explosion above the atomsphere over the centre of Western Europe could have damaging effects to unprotected electrical and electronic equipment over much of the NATO area . . .'[4] How costly, effective or common protection is, I do not know. But the possible disruption of military and civil activities in the absence of protection looks alarming. After the civil defence exercise 'Square Leg' in Britain in the summer of 1980 it was reported that 'Communications used in the exercise yesterday are not proof against electro-magnetic pulse, the sudden and potentially destructive surge of power which comes after a nuclear explosion.'[5]

(b) 'Another unexpected effect of high-altitude bursts was the blackout of high frequency radio communications. Disruption of the ionosphere (which reflects radio signals back to the earth) by nuclear bursts over the Pacific has wiped out long-distance radio communications for hours at distances up to 600 miles from the burst point.'[6] Or as it is put in more technical terms in the WEU Report, the ionization of the atmosphere and ionosphere ' . . . can cause serious interference with radio communications and the functioning of radar when burst height is above 15 km, the effects increasing with height of burst above 15 km. The high frequency and very high frequency radio bands are most affected; other frequencies are unlikely to be disturbed for very long.'[7]

This appears to be a full catalogue of the possible direct effects of a *single* nuclear weapon. Since there have been more than a thousand weapon tests, it should be fairly reliable. But one must be careful in using it for the following reasons:-

(i) Some of the effects – e.g. the extent of fallout and the electro-magnetic effects – were discovered by accident. As the ACDA Report puts it, 'Much of our knowledge was thus gained by chance – a fact which should imbue us with humility as we contemplate the remaining uncertainties (as well as the certainties) about nuclear warfare.'[8]

(ii) The extent of the death, injury and destruction caused by, say, a weapon falling upon a city will depend upon the cumulative effects of fire, the disorganization of the normal facilities for life, and presence of innumerable dead, burnt and irradiated people in radioactive surroundings. Explosions on uninhabited test grounds provide no direct evidence of these effects. Only Hiroshima and Nagasaki can give us any direct indication of what might happen.

(iii) A nuclear war in which many weapons were let off would multiply these effects and produce reactions and cumulative effects, some of which can be foreseen but the totality of which we can foresee no better than a writer of morbid science fiction.

38

Hiroshima and Nagasaki

The bombs at Hiroshima and Nagasaki were tiny by modern standards. Their explosive power was in the range 10-20 kt. The Hiroshima bomb is often put, more precisely, at 13 kt., the Nagasaki bomb at 20 kt. The radius of blast damage will have been about one-eighth or less of that for a 1 mt. bomb: i.e. the radii for the circles of damage given in Table 3 for a 1 mt. weapon can be divided by eight to see the effects of a 20 kt. bomb. For heat effects, the reduction in the circles would be less.

United States estimates of casualties at Hiroshima and Nagasaki, made in the 1940s and early 1950s, are shown in Table 4. Japanese estimates broadly agree on the percentage casualty rates at different distances from the explosion, which are our prime concern, but they put higher figures on the total population in each town and hence on the absolute number of casualties: 140,000 dead at Hiroshima by the end of December 1945 and 70,000 at Nagasaki.[9]

The key results are:

(a) Within 0.6 miles from the explosion about 95 per cent of the population was killed or injured in both towns, the vast majority killed, but not all immediately. (The equivalent distance for a 1 mt. weapon is 2.6 miles.)

(b) 'It has been estimated that some 50 per cent of deaths were caused by burns of one kind or another, but this figure is only a rough estimate. Close to two-thirds of those who died at Hiroshima during the first day after the explosion were reported to have been badly burned. In addition, there were many deaths from burns during the first week.'[10]

(c) Because the bombs at Hiroshima and Nagasaki were airburst, casualties due to fallout were completely absent.[11]

(d) In a circle of radius 0.6 to 1.6 miles, the population of Nagasaki was low and the ground hilly, compared with Hiroshima. The total population exposed to the bomb was therefore less at Nagasaki than at Hiroshima, and so consequently were total casualties, despite the greater size of the Nagasaki bomb.

39

Table 4: *Casualties at Hiroshima and Nagasaki*

| Circle (radius) | Population | | Casualties | | Casualty Rate |
	Number	Density per sq. mile	Killed	Injured	
HIROSHIMA					
0.0 to 0.6 miles	31,200	25,800	26,700	3,000	95%
0.6 to 1.6 miles	144,800	22,700	39,600	53,000	64%
1.6 to 3.1 miles	80,300	3,500	1,700	20,000	27%
Totals	256,300	8,500	68,000	76,000	56%
NAGASAKI					
0.0 to 0.6	30,900	25,500	27,200	1,900	94%
0.6 to 1.6	27,700	4,400	9,500	8,100	64%
1.6 to 3.1	115,200	5,100	1,300	11,000	11%
Totals	173,800	5,800	38,000	21,000	34%

Source: The effects of Nuclear Weapons, ed. Samuel Glasstone and Philip J. Dolan, U.S. Dept. of Defense and U.S. Dept. of Energy, Third Edition, reprinted February 1977, p. 544.

(e) At Hiroshima, with its larger flat area of dense buildings, the area severely damaged by fire was four times as great as at Nagasaki and there developed a firestorm, a phenomenon which Nagasaki escaped:[12] a wind blew from all directions into the burning area, reaching a velocity of 30 to 40 mph two to three hours after the explosion and dropping again six hours after. 'The high winds are produced largely by the updraft of the heated air over an extensive burning area. They are thus the equivalent, on a very large scale, of the draft of a chimney under which a fire is burning.'[13] The result in Hiroshima, as in German and Japanese cities where firestorms were caused by incendiary bombs in World War II, was that the winds ensured that everything combustible within that area was destroyed in a fire lasting many hours. Moreover within the area of a firestorm the roasting and asphyxiation of people in shelters becomes a cause of death additional to all the others at work.[14]

(f) At Hiroshima, 70 per cent of the fire-fighting equipment was crushed in the collapse of fire stations; 80 per cent of the fire-fighting personnel were unable to respond; streets were blocked; the water pressure failed because of broken pipes and mains.[15]

(g) 'Before the bomb, there were 150 doctors alive and functioning in Hiroshima; after, 65 were dead and most of the rest were wounded. The statistics for nurses were equally grim: before the bomb 1,780 were alive and functioning; after, 1,654 were dead or too badly hurt to work.'[16] Severe burns require the most labour-intensive care by nurses, as well as large quantities of blood, plasma, dressings and other medical supplies. A normal hospital can cope with very few severe burn cases.

(h) Radiation affected the blood count of survivors severely for several months and so increased their vulnerability to disease.

(i) 2,279 names of people who died in the past year, 1979/80, the thirty-fifth since the bomb was dropped on Hiroshima, were recently added to the list of deaths officially attributed to the explosion since 1952. There are now 97,964 names on the list. *The Times* reported from Tokyo that 'More than 200,000 people have probably perished since the explosion, but it has never been possible to work out precise figures.'[17] Clearly it must be increasingly hard as the years go by to know whether to attribute a death to the bomb or to other causes. The figures may be wrong. But the point they illustrate stands, that deaths from cancer and other causes will continue for many years amongst the victims of a nuclear explosion.

(j) In relation to the size of the bomb, the number of casualties from flash burns was high at Hiroshima and Nagasaki, where many people were in the open, wearing light summer clothing which afforded little protection from burns, and the sky was clear.[18]

The Effects of Many Weapons

We now reach the realm of modelling and conjecture about hypothetical events. There is no experience to go by.

In the United States, the ACDA Report *The Effects of Nuclear War,* published in April 1979, describes the results of 'large scale computer war game simulations of general nuclear war between the United States and the Soviet Union' in which 'several attack scenarios were analyzed using the strategic forces projected for the United States and the Soviet Union under a SALT TWO agreement. The scenarios assumed a heavy Soviet first strike against U.S. strategic forces (ICBM silos, bomber bases and submarine bases), against other U.S. military installations, and against U.S. industry. The U.S. would then retaliate with its surviving forces against a similar set of Soviet targets.'[19]

The populations of the two countries were generally not directly aimed at but, since they tend to be located within range of the effects of weapons aimed at military and industrial targets, casualties were colossal. For *each* of the two countries, the estimate of damage of the more direct kinds was as follows:

Deaths within 30 days	25 to 100 million
Industrial damage	65% to 90% destroyed
Cities	200 largest cities destroyed. 80% of all cities of 25,000 inhabitants or more attacked by at least one weapon.

After 30 days, 'many more would die from disease, starvation and other causes.'[20]

In the simulated retaliatory attack on the Soviet Union, no less than about 60 warheads 'went down within the Moscow city limits, which would be typical of a major nuclear exchange'. This represents about 1,400 times the megatonnage used on Hiroshima and Nagasaki. The direct nuclear radiation alone would reach such huge levels all over the city that people who were 'very well sheltered could have some chance if they stayed inside for *several months*' [my underlining]. Blast and fire would cover almost the whole city. Assuming no firestorm, 85 to 90 per cent of urban housing would be destroyed. The same fate would befall New York.

Assuming that half the weapons were groundburst, vast areas would be covered by fallout of an intensity that is lethal to the unprotected; very large areas would be covered by such large doses of fallout that more than half the people who stayed in basements would die from radiation.

There is then a list of indirect effects. Here uncertainty increases. The effects listed are a massive long-lasting *housing shortage;* an immediate *lack of water and food stocks,* which would compel people to leave shelter and expose themselves to radiation; *loss of crops and livestock* from blast and fallout; possible *damage to the ozone layer,* causing an increase in ultraviolet rays for several years throughout the northern hemisphere and hence widespread injury to people and animals, and possibly a climatic change that would damage agriculture; *disease* caused by the presence of millions of corpses of humans and animals, by reduced resistance to disease on account of radiation, by poor sanitation, crowding, lack of medical supplies and food, plus a long-run increase in cancer due to radiation and ultraviolet burning; *radiation hot spots* to be detected and isolated; effects on the *aquatic environment; genetic effects* about which there is much uncertainty but 'There would be an increased rate of genetic deformities and many people would be affected on a worldwide basis';[21] the problem of organizing life in the *post-attack environment* where communication, transport and the facilities of life are destroyed; and finally the problem of *economic recovery,* the restoration of law and order and the likelihood that 'the reconstruction of pre-attack property and financial rights may be almost impossible'.

Nobody, so far as I know, has challenged the broad picture conveyed by this report as to the *magnitude* of the direct effects of an all-out nuclear war between the Soviet Union and the United States nor the *nature* of the indirect effects listed.

There have, however, been arguments about the effects of nuclear war.

Twenty years ago Herman Kahn argued at length,[22] on the basis of a huge structure of questionable assumptions, that the United States could survive an all-out nuclear exchange with the nuclear arsenals he predicted for the 1970s (over 2,000 bombs dropped on the United States) and make a fairly rapid recovery. This was in the context of arguing that expenditure on civil defence, offering a prospect of meaningful survival, was necessary to make nuclear deterrence credible: you can't credibly threaten to use nuclear weapons unless you are in a position to survive their use by your opponent. His argument was heavily criticized.[23] One telling criticism was that only a few years later he argued that in an all-out nuclear war the Russians 'unless their strike had been extraordinarily successful . . . would be likely simply to disappear as a nation – or at least to be set back 25 to 100 years in industrial and material wealth'.[24]

Kahn's kind of argument is revived periodically in less extreme form, for example in England now, by those who seek to make deterrence seem a credible policy to their enemy or a reasonable one to their own people. Conversely, there have been occasional stories from the military in the West that the Soviet Union has spent so much on civil defence that she could withstand a nuclear war unless even more weapons are bought by the West. All this smacks of wishful thinking by militarists.

Then there have been the major studies commissioned by United States Government agencies and undertaken by groups of American scientists. One was the 1975 Report *Long-term Worldwide Effects of Multiple Nuclear Weapons Detonations* undertaken by the National Academy of Sciences at the initiative of the United States Arms Control and Disarmament Agency. Another has been the recent report, *The Effects of Nuclear War*, by the Office of Technology Assessment of the U.S. Congress.[25] This includes a useful comparison of the various estimates of the effects of nuclear war made by different agencies of the United States Government.

The third strand in the argument are articles and statements by people who have questioned whether the official scenarios do not understate the possible consequences of nuclear war. Thus Beaumont, emphasizing the uncertainty about what would happen, argues that 'From nuclear testing there has emerged a body of knowledge, a *corpus thermonuclearum*. It is comprised of surmise, guess, arbitrary weightings, acronyms, catchphrases, polemic and equations. Academics have built careers and reputations as advocates or opponents of the complex, as modifiers of scenarios, or as inventors of new phrases.'[26] He then reminds us of some of the huge past errors of the military and their civilian advisers, including those relating to bombing in World War II and the conduct of military operations in Vietnam. And he then lists some of the possible consequences of nuclear war that cannot readily be assessed: broken pipelines, fallen power lines, spills of oil, of chemicals, of nuclear waste and toxins; forest fires, floods; the possibility of induced earthquakes; the spillage of fissile material from one's own weapons hit on the ground by pre-emptive strikes; the contamination of the sea as weapon-bearing submarines are attacked.

Hemingway, having emphasized the risk of disease after an all-out nuclear war, discusses the psychological effects at Hiroshima: a sense of an overwhelming encounter with death led, amongst the survivors, to a deadening of emotional reactions to what was happening around them and to behaviour which impeded recovery: a recovery which was achieved by the efforts of people from other unbombed areas of Japan, not by local survivors.[27] Crimes of violence and theft all increased to an extraordinary extent, if Hemingway's figures are reliable; and so apparently did resort to drink and drugs. He then mentions some of the possible ecological consequences of nuclear war: a Hudson Institute scenario recounted by Barry Commoner suggests that in a farming area 80 per cent of adult birds and nearly all young ones are killed by fallout, and farming is disrupted, with the result that the insect population increases so much that nearly half the region's crops would be lost; or forest fires caused by nuclear weapons lead to deforestation so that rainfall, instead of being retained in the ground, floods off the land causing soil

45

erosion and leaving empty river beds in dry seasons, as in any desert area. In the nature of the case, the writers of this second group are more alarming: their object is to utter warnings.

Finally, mention should be made of a group of distinguished American medical scientists who at a recent symposium at the Harvard Medical School examined what would happen if one 20 mt. bomb were to land on Boston. According to a report in *Science*, 'The unanimous conclusion of the speakers was that no adequate medical response would be possible even in the event of a "limited" nuclear exchange, and that civil defense plans are nothing more than a dangerous illusion.'[28] They sent telegrams to President Carter and Mr Brezhnev warning that medical disaster planning for nuclear war is 'meaningless', that 'there is no effective civil defense' and that 'recovery from a nuclear war would be next to impossible'. They appear to have gathered a considerable following in the United States.

The notable difference between the official reports on the effects of a nuclear war which we have cited and the reported views of this Harvard symposium is that the former, while stating the radii of destruction of different kinds and other facts, say very little about the fate of the injured or the fate of those in shelters. They seem to avoid anything which indicates directly the probable futility of relying on civil defence and medical services. In two chilling sentences, the report on the Harvard symposium fills the gap: 'Bomb shelters would become ovens. There would be about 10,000 severe burn cases in Boston – unmanageable even if medical personnel and facilities were left intact, since the whole country has no more than 1,000 intensive burn-care beds.'

Other Studies
Studies in Germany, notably the massive work by Carl Friedrich von Weizsäcker, have concluded that even a brief and local war in which nuclear weapons stationed in Europe were used would cause millions of deaths and destroy Western Germany.[29]

Lord Zuckerman has recently reminded us that in Britain it was concluded in the 1950s, when nuclear arsenals were much smaller, that there was no means of protecting the population against the consequences of nuclear war, a proposition which was set out in the Defence White Paper of 1957; and that British

46

studies of the consequences of an all-out nuclear war confirmed the view that in the North American and Eurasiatic continents there would be 'hundreds of millions killed in a flash, and with most of those who were not so lucky then dying of the effects of radiation, of starvation, without medical or any other help'.[30]

Similar results have been found in other studies.

Conclusion

The conclusion is inescapable that nuclear war would be an experience of the utmost horror. A common fate would be death from untended burns, radiation sickness, broken limbs, disease, starvation, thirst and other forms of suffering, rather than the instant death one is tempted to envisage.

Whether human life would survive, or civilization as we know it be restored after an interval, no one can say with certainty. We could know that only after the event, if we survived.

5   The Mechanics of the Arms Race

No one can look at the present accumulation of destructive power without questioning the sanity of those who brought it into being. How has it happened?

The Arms Race

We cannot explain the nuclear arms race any better than we can explain anything else in history. But we can say something.

As a starting point there is the classic model of an arms race as an 'action-reaction' mechanism: once two nations, or groups of nations, become rivals and begin to arm against each other, for any mixture of offensive and defensive motives, they will be led to compete with one another in the acquisition of arms. Usually the result has been war. The arms race leading up to 1914 is an example.

This explains a good deal. Yet on its own it is an explanation that is too mechanistic and apolitical. It does not explain what starts an arms race, what dictates its pace or what determines the chances of a peaceful political ending to it.

In the strategic theorizing which accompanied the growth of nuclear arsenals in the United States in the 1950s and early 1960s there was developed, in the concept of deterrence, a notion of what level of arms was sufficient and therefore how many nuclear weapons a nation, behaving rationally, should acquire; there was a notion of what should constrain the race. The argument runs essentially as follows: postulate two 'rational' creatures in conflict with each other. (To which you may ask, 'Why should they be unable to settle their conflict if they are rational?', only to be told that it is a possibility we must cater for or some other answer which casts doubt on the meaning of the word rational.) Given the assumed nature of these creatures, usually called 'players' since the model derives from games theory, they are deterred from attacking one another only by the threat that unacceptable damage by nuclear weapons will be inflicted on their civilian populations. The civilian population is chosen, despite laws of war and moral considerations to the contrary, on the grounds that an attack on it is what hurts most and so deters most effectively. If one side ceases to maintain the capacity to inflict unacceptable damage on the other, it risks being attacked – or being threatened with attack and compelled to concede whatever is demanded of it because it knows it would be unable to deter its enemy. The conclusion is that you need to arm, i.e. to race with your opponent, only to the point where you maintain the capacity to inflict unacceptable damage on him. This defines the 'minimum deterrent' or 'minimum assured destruction capability' that you need maintain.

If one asks how many weapons are needed for a minimum deterrent, I know of no better answer than that provided years ago by the American, Mr McGeorge Bundy, shortly after leaving his post as Special Assistant to the President for National Security Affairs:

> In the real world of real political leaders – whether here or in the Soviet Union   a decision that would bring even one hydrogen bomb on one city of one's own country would be recognized in advance as a catastrophic blunder; ten bombs on ten cities would be a disaster beyond history; and a hundred bombs on a hundred cities are unthinkable. [1]

Clearly present nuclear arsenals, running to tens of thousands of nuclear weapons, vastly exceed the requirements of a minimum deterrent as perceived by Bundy. There is huge 'overkill'.

To see how these vastly excessive nuclear arsenals came about it is necessary to try to distinguish between

(a) the strategic arguments that have been used to justify their acquisition; and

(b) the political, economic and technological forces which cause the military, the arms industry, the weapons scientists and politicians to push for more weapons and to invent or embrace the strategic arguments under (a).

49

Strategic arguments

In the United States, where these matters are debated publicly, a variety of arguments has been used to justify the acquisition of more nuclear weapons – or later, the possession of the huge arsenals that result – whilst always maintaining that deterrence is the ultimate objective.

First there are four arguments which are logically consistent with deterrence being the only objective:

(a) To attribute to the Soviet Union, rightly or wrongly, the ability successfully to knock out a high proportion of American weapons before they can be launched (a 'first-strike capability') or the ability to defend itself against American weapons after they are launched by means of anti-aircraft or anti-ballistic missile defences, so that the fraction of American weapons which can be expected to reach their targets is diminished. This argument was first propounded by Wohlstetter in his famous article, 'The Delicate Balance of Terror',[2] based on a RAND study which suggested that American long-range bombers sitting on aerodromes, which were then the prime delivery vehicles for United States nuclear weapons, would be highly vulnerable to a Soviet first strike, once the Soviets developed substantial nuclear forces. There followed the pursuit of invulnerable ballistic missiles in submarines or silos. It has subsequently been argued with increasing plausibility that various Soviet missiles possess the combination of accuracy and yield needed for a first-strike capability i.e. one of their weapons would have a high probability of knocking out an American one. Similarly, there have been stories about Soviet ABM defences, some of which appear to have been well-founded, some ill-founded (the Talin line).

(b) To raise your estimates or forecasts of Soviet forces, sometimes with a wild degree of exaggeration as in the case of the bomber and missile gaps, sometimes with some underestimation, as happened with respect to delivery vehicles, but not warheads, subsequently.

(c) To raise your estimate of the amount of punishment with which you need to threaten the Soviet Union in order to deter it from aggression, and hence the number of weapons you must be confident about delivering despite failures and enemy defences (the 'minimum assured destruction capability'). This was done explicitly in the time of Mr McNamara, when the Department of Defense's 'Posture Statement', the equivalent of the British Defence White Paper, spelt out an amazing catalogue of the casualties and damage with which it was said to be necessary to threaten the Soviet Union in order to deter it.

The fact that the United States had acquired a huge arsenal of nuclear weapons on the basis of the bomber and missile gaps must help to explain why this extravagant doctrine – and some of the other arguments listed here – was publicly embraced at that time.

(d) To use 'worst-case' analysis when calculating how many weapons you need to satisfy the requirements dictated by the considerations we have listed so far. That is, you combine the most pessimistic assumptions about the failure rate of your weapons, the losses inflicted by enemy defences and so on, with the most optimistic assumptions (from the point of view of your opponent) about the performance and success of his weapons in killing yours. This is done in the name of conservatism or caution, but is clearly a way of fuelling the action-reaction process. If the Soviets do likewise and seek to match the United States, there may be a great increase in arms levels before both sides are satisfied.

There are then arguments which do not fit strictly within the framework of deterrence and which imply the pursuit of objectives other than deterrence. Here there have been two alternative strategies that have mattered. One is the 'flexible response', meaning the strategy of stationing tactical missiles under United States control in Europe and planning to use those first in the event of a successful Soviet conventional attack, holding strategic weapons in reserve. The second is the 'counter-force' strategy, sometimes called a 'damage-limiting' strategy, meaning that you keep nuclear weapons for the purpose of attacking your enemy's nuclear weapons – in addition to those you keep for the purpose of making punitive attacks on his cities for purposes of deterrence. Both strategies mean that you prepare to fight a war with nuclear weapons, instead of holding them only as a deterrent.

And then there has been the corruption of the notion of deterrence into a notion of balance. Balance, referred to as a balance of power, a balance of forces or a balance of terror, is a much older, looser concept and is perhaps all the more effective politically for that reason. It is different from deterrence in one crucial respect: it sets no absolute limit to how many weapons you must possess, only the relative limit that you must not have less than your opponent; hence it can be used to justify an arms race without limit. It is said or implied that, *regardless* of how many weapons you have, balance is required for deterrence; and then the pursuit of balance merges into the pursuit of nuclear superiority as a symbol of political strength – and its counterpart, the avoidance of inferiority as a sign of political weakness. Whether superiority or inferiority really makes any difference to international bargaining power is open to question, as we shall see in Chapter 9.

Since the pursuit of balance and of war-fighting capabilities are increasingly important, they are discussed in more detail in Chapter 6.

On the Soviet side, the strategic arguments used to justify the acquisition of weapons are not as openly known and debated as they are in the United States. But a certain amount is published on strategic doctrine. From this it appears that the Soviet Union has never directly espoused a doctrine of deterrence by threatening unacceptable punishment – though the fact that appalling damage would occur if nuclear arsenals were used has been emphasized. Rather the Soviet Union has taken the line that it would not use nuclear weapons first but that if its enemies resorted to them it would respond by using its weapons to cripple their ability to fight i.e. attack their forces, bases, communication and supply system and war industries.

The Politico-Economic Forces
The politico-economic forces generating the arms race are not fully understood, but they are of supreme importance.

First, there is the pressure of technology. With the discovery of nuclear weapons, scientists were given almost limitless budgets with which to pursue the development of nuclear weapons and to explore any areas where the application of science and technology to military ends might give a nation a comparative advantage. In the United States one can see nakedly that the approach has been to think of any way in which science and technology might be harnessed for military purposes and pursue it on the grounds that, if we can think of it, so can they; and if they may do it, we must do so. The blame for this lies as much with the scientists and technologists as with the military or the politicians. Once scientists accept the notion that the development of means of destruction helps to ensure peace via deterrence (or, in old-fashioned terms, a balance of power), competition between patriotic scientists within a nation can soon lead to a proliferation of ideas and requests for funds. The greater the funds that are granted, the more extravagant will be the ideas that are pursued.

Major steps in the arms race can be seen to have occurred when major new weapons systems have been devised and are ready to be accepted or rejected. As Elizabeth Young once put it, new weapons systems grow until they are ripe plums. At that stage strong pressures to accept them come from the scientists who developed them, the firms who hope to produce them and the military who hope to gain strength, modernity and prestige from acquiring them. The cruise missile is a topical example.

Secondly, it is clear that international actions not directly related to nuclear weapons spasmodically influence the pace of the nuclear arms race. In the early post-war years, the Soviet colonization of eastern Europe, the Berlin Blockade and the Korean War all alarmed the West and contributed to its pursuit of nuclear weapons. Once the Korean War was over, Stalin had gone and Khrushchev was in power, the arms race cooled down. There were unilateral reductions in military spending by both superpowers, and there seemed a chance for disarmament. But that was lost. And then Kennedy hotted things up. His huge missile programmes based on the missile gap must have helped provoke Khrushchev to place medium-range nuclear missiles in Cuba in 1962, when the Soviet Union was very inferior in long-range weapons – the action that led to the Cuban crisis in which the superpowers came to the brink of nuclear war. After that, Kennedy's decision to commit the United States to war in Vietnam, and the subsequent increase in the scale and brutality of United States actions there, must have frightened the Soviets and reinforced the position of their 'hawks' *vis-à-vis* their 'doves' in debates about nuclear weapons policy and other matters. More recently the Soviet invasion of Afghanistan has had a similar effect in the West, notably in the United States and Britain.

Thirdly, there is the whole complex of domestic politico-economic pressures. It was President Eisenhower, a Republican president and ex-Supreme Allied Commander, who in January 1961, when his term of office as President was ending and Kennedy was about to succeed him, warned the Americans to guard against the acquisition of unwarranted influence, whether sought or unsought, by the 'military-industrial complex' that had come into being since World War II. His words are reproduced in full in Appendix B.

Since then a lot has been written about the military-industrial complex. It is well established that the United States military raises alarms about the Soviet threat regularly when it presents its budget and seeks more money for new weapons programmes. When the annual posture statement and defence budget are presented, Washington journalists report the game almost like an annual sporting event. It is also well established that the firms supplying arms, notably the aerospace firms, are very active in the United States in proposing new weapons, bidding for new weapons programmes and generally furthering their commercial interests in the closest possible co-operation with the military. And together the military, the arms-supplying firms and their specialized journals (which live on advertizing by the firms supplying arms and their components) are extemely effective in public relations. In this they enjoy special advantages: they play upon fear and patriotism, two strong emotions, and they possess and can manipulate secret information about a secretive adversary, the Soviet Union – though the openness of the United States Government means that rival streams of information may be fed by hawks and doves in the official world to their respective supporters outside.

In the Soviet Union, the political framework is very different and public political debate about policy is negligible. Yet within their secretive system they must have many of the same arguments as their counterparts in the United States; and a military-industrial complex, similar to, though not the same as,

54

that in the United States, must have grown up during the arms race.[3]

Competition between politicians *within* nations has been important, as well as competition *between* nations. In the West, one can see that this is not confined to one political party but occurs, in different ways, on the Right and Left.

On the Right, there are politicians who have adopted the posture of the patriotic strong leader seeking to rally the nation to traditional values, to check left-wing tendencies and to reinforce law and order at home. They have proclaimed that they will restore the greatness of the nation and that for this purpose they will increase its military strength, which has been neglected by their political opponents. They usually invoke and emphasize the Soviet threat as part of their general rallying cry. Examples are Mr Reagan and Barry Goldwater (an extreme case); Mrs Thatcher, Herr Strauss of Germany and earlier General de Gaulle – though he, rather than playing up the Soviet threat, insisted that France should have her own nuclear forces so as not to be at the mercy of the United States.

On the Left, there is the phenomenon of the 'liberal hawk', the member of the left-wing party who, in seeking to be respectable and to appeal to centre voters whose support is necessary for the election of his party, wishes to insure himself against being labelled 'soft on the Commies', an accusation which his right-wing opponent will delight in throwing at him. He therefore plays up the Soviet threat and advocates 'strength' vehemently. The best example is Kennedy, a Democrat, who accused his predecessor, Eisenhower, a Republican, of neglecting the defences of the United States; who campaigned on the missile gap, adopted huge missile programmes after he knew the gap was false – and committed the United States to the Vietnam War.

In the United States, it is not just the electorate to whom the politicians must pay attention. The Joint Chiefs of Staff make official pronouncements to the Congress and the public, giving their views on nuclear policy, and the President needs their support if he is to get his policies through the Congress.

To read one of the statements of the Chairman of the Joint Chiefs of Staff that accompany the annual United States Defense Budget is a startling experience to an Englishman used to the notion that the military should be silent while still on the active payroll, and should certainly keep out of politics. The latest annual statement by the Chairman of the Joint Chiefs I have to hand is that made in 1979 with reference to the year 1980. It is entitled 'Military Posture and National Power'. It addresses the whole performance of the United States relative to the Soviet Union, including economic performance, political appeal and other matters. It reads like a Victorian headmaster summing up the performance of the school at the end of the academic year and telling the boys they must do better if they are not to be outstripped by the rival school. It is taken absolutely for granted that the pursuit of 'power' is what matters to the United States, that it is appropriate for a military man to give his views of the world economic and military situation seen from that point of view, and that it is appropriate for him to say:

> In closing, I would suggest that increased United States defense spending should be only one element in a more confident and assertive national strategy. I believe this country has the wisdom and the vision to wield all the elements of its power in a constructive fashion, without being arrogant or provocative.

The statement of the Secretary of Defense is similar, as it is almost bound to be. Both he and the Chairman of the Joint Chiefs are putting forward the same budget, and by that stage they should have sorted out any differences they had in preparing it. But the Secretary of Defense's statement is the less militant of the two. He does not call for a 'more assertive national strategy' or anything like that. Moreover he makes one most revealing remark. Having said that 'the United States, fortunately, is by most measures the strongest nation in the world' and then referred to the dangers of being too dependent on oil, he says:

> Among our international problems the Soviet Union undoubtedly looms as by far the principal adversary player.

His use of the word 'player' suddenly suggests that he is engaged in a game, not in a real conflict; the game clearly is the competitive accumulation of nuclear and other weapons.

To sum up, one can see how in the United States the various

competitive forces let loose in the arms race have reinforced one another in a circular and cumulative process in which nuclear arsenals have spiralled to their present level and are still rising, and in which weapons have become ever more sophisticated and baroque in their extravagance.[4] Nuclear arms have become symbols of 'strength'. The pursuit of superior strength and the avoidance of 'inferiority' have become political compulsions in a militarized political ethos bred by the arms race itself. Decisions to take the next step in the race are always by reference to what weapons the other superpower is currently acquiring or is expected to acquire. So they are always short-sighted. No one steps in to ask how the race will end.

6 Strategic Trends and their Dangers

It is always tempting to become engrossed in the particular steps that are currently being taken in the nuclear arms race. The latest devices are usually fascinating for their futuristic technology. And the exciting issue of policy at each round in the arms race is which weapon to acquire and what effect its acquisition will have on nuclear strategy.

But it is important to stand back. Otherwise you lose sight of both the political and economic forces generating the arms race, and of the direction in which the risks of war are being driven by the advance of technology and strategy. It is the latter which concerns us here: what are the continuing trends of technology and strategy against which current steps should be seen?

The most important phenomenon has been the drift of strategy away from simple deterrence towards preparations for nuclear warfare. This has occurred over quite a long period in two ways noted earlier: the adoption of a counter-force strategy by the United States towards the Soviet Union and, very probably, by the Soviet Union towards the United States; and the adoption by NATO of the strategy of the 'flexible response' in Europe.

Counter-force strategy

Since only two nuclear weapons have ever been used in war, and that happened 35 years ago, strategic doctrines relating to the use of large numbers of weapons are based on speculation, model-making and war games. They have never been tested in practice. Nevertheless they are at the heart of the making and presentation of policy for the acquisition of weapons and their planned use (or 'targetting'). Causation runs in several directions. Doctrine will influence the choice of weapons to be developed and acquired. The weapons proposed and developed by the scientists and technologists will influence doctrine: those promoting a weapon will suggest a doctrine to justify and rationalize its acquisition;

and each branch of the armed forces will produce doctrines to justify the continued acquisition of the type of weapons in which they specialize: the Air Force will produce doctrines justifying aircraft and land-based missiles (if, as in the United States, they man those weapons) and so on.

In the United States, and in other western countries which, derivatively, follow the same style of strategic debate, the three basic strategic notions relating to nuclear weapons, as noted in Chapter 5, have been deterrence, balance and counter-force.

Deterrence, as noted previously, means threatening to inflict unacceptable damage on the civilian population of your enemy if he oversteps some mark. It requires few weapons which are, so far as possible, invulnerable to enemy attack and only accurate enough to hit large cities – the targets against which punishment would be wrought. The theory suggests that both sides can simultaneously deter the other by having the required number of invulnerable weapons; and that there will then be a stable balance of forces through the 'mutual assured destruction' (MAD) capability. Measures which are believed to enhance this capability have been called 'stabilizing', meaning that they are expected to reassure the other side.

The pursuit of balance not only removes any absolute limit on how many nuclear weapons you need, it also leaves open the possibility of subdividing your arsenal and claiming the need to achieve balance, avoid inferiority or get ahead in more and more categories and sub-categories of nuclear weapon. The category 'long-range theatre weapons' is a recent example.

A counter-force strategy means planning to attack the nuclear forces of your enemy so as to reduce, or ideally eliminate, his ability to attack you. It requires that you possess a large number of warheads relative to the number of launching points of your enemy; that you know where his weapons are; and that your warheads are sufficiently accurate in relation to their explosive power to destroy his weapons (which will be hardened against attack, for example, in buried concrete silos).

In theory, both sides can simultaneously possess a counter-force capability. If one side believes the other side to possess a counter-force capability, it may become dangerously trigger-happy: for upon getting evidence of enemy missiles approaching, it will have only a few minutes in which to launch its weapons before they may be destroyed. Steps which are believed to produce a counter-force capability undermine deterrence. They have been called 'destabilizing'; they have been regarded as offensive and likely to alarm rather than reassure the other side.

The strategic policy of the United States, which NATO has always endorsed willingly or reluctantly, can best be described as a shifting mixture of deterrence, balance and counter-force. The pursuit of balance (usually implying the pursuit of superiority by one or both sides) is evident from the numbers of weapons accumulated by both sides and from the reasons for their accumulation which we have looked at earlier. It is the movement towards a counter-force strategy and the acquisition of weapons of the quality required for that strategy which concern us here.

There appear to be three main reasons for the trend in the United States to a counter-force capability (or 'war-fighting capability' as it is sometimes called).

Firstly, there has for a long time been a counter-force school centred on the United States Air Force. An American, Arthur Waskow, recounted in a paper presented to a conference in 1961 that Air Force strategists reacted to the Soviet acquisition of thermo-nuclear weapons and delivery systems in the 1950s, 'not by deciding it meant thermonuclear war was too dangerous for the United States to consider, but by working out a refinement of thermonuclear war which they hoped would not be too dangerous. Thus counter-force theory was born, from consultation among Air Force officers, some scholars on contract to the Air Force through the RAND Corporation, and officials in industries serving Air Force needs. The theory was tailored to fit the characteristics of weapons the Air Force either already had or was looking forward to having.'[1]

Mr Waskow then went on, twenty years ago, to describe an Air Force strategy which foreshadows precisely the counter-force strategy recently proclaimed publicly by President Carter. His description is worth quoting at length:

The Air Force suggests war is most likely to start through the Soviet Bloc's launching a major atomic strike at the United States, attempting to knock out as much as possible of the American atomic striking force. With what was left of its

60

atomic forces, the United States would have to return the blow. The major decision would be whether to retaliate against Communist cities or forces. But an attack against cities would leave enemy atomic forces intact for a second blow, and this blow would come against American cities in revenge for the annihilation of Communist cities. Since American cities cannot be adequately protected from H-bomb attack, such a return blow would destroy American society. For that reason, the Air Force would aim the American retaliatory attack at Soviet atomic missile and bomber bases, hoping to smash as much as possible of the Soviet thermonuclear capability without destroying Soviet society.

The hope would be that this American return strike would reduce the enemy atomic forces below the threshold of continued capability to act effectively. If enough American atomic capability remained to threaten enemy cities effectively, the United States could demand and receive a surrender. If the American atomic force were also knocked out of commission, the war would end in a stalemate and would preserve a going, if somewhat damaged, American society. But if the enemy, by striking first, had incapacitated the American atomic force while preserving it own effectiveness, the United States might have to surrender.

Counter-force strategists argue that the initial Communist attack would be directed at American forces, not cities, for reasons that are a mirror image of American reasons for striking back at forces, not cities. In other words, the Communists would fear that an attack upon American cities that left American forces intact would be punished by a direct attack on their cities that would destroy their society. Counter-force theorists therefore argue that each side would find it to its own interest to restrict its attack extremely carefully.

This belief in self-control leads counter-force strategists to insist that American society would not be irreparably damaged by such a war. These strategists estimate that up to 30 million Americans might die in such a war, but they regard this as an acceptable blow. They believe that after absorbing such a blow the United States (and Communist governments also) would continue to be able to act by carefully rationalistic calculations in an attempt to minimize destruction. They believe it likely that neither side would try to destroy the other's capital and government, since each side would want to have the other's authorities intact, able to negotiate or surrender.[2]

He goes on to explain how the United States Navy favoured a capacity for massive retaliation against cities, for which its Polaris submarines would be suited, whilst the Army favoured the development of a limited warfare capability, for which its forces were suited, and how these two services together favoured these two strategies in combination, i.e. what came to be called the flexible response. The nuclear weapons policy actually adopted was a mixture of the rival strategies – counter-force, counter-city and limited war – which kept the three services happy.

A second reason for the adoption of a counter-force strategy was that as more and more weapons were accumulated, there were far more warheads than there were cities to hit, so that some were aimed inevitably at military targets, including Soviet nuclear weapons.

A third reason is that technical innovations have made, and are making, a counter-force strategy increasingly feasible. Missiles have been given multiple warheads (which increases the ratio of targets you can aim at relative to launching points vulnerable to attack); missiles have been made increasingly accurate (which, as we have seen, greatly reduces the size of weapon required to destroy by blast a given target); warheads have been made more efficient in terms of yield to weight and they have been made better able to penetrate defences and survive 'fratricide' (destruction of one of your weapons by another launched by your own side which goes off in its vicinity).

On the other hand, innovations that would improve invulnerability have been limited. Silos in which land-based missiles are placed cannot be hardened to the point where they will survive a nuclear attack of high accuracy.

The first official declaration that a counter-force strategy had been adopted by the United States was made by Mr McNamara in a famous speech at Ann Arbor in June 1962, when the United States, after the missile gap, knew that it enjoyed marked superiority in strategic missiles. It is impossible to say how far the proponents of the counter-force strategy had caused the large missile orders and how far the acquisition of so many missiles caused the official adoption of the strategy, but the link between strength and the adoption of the strategy is evident from the words used by Mr McNamara:

> The US has come to the conclusion that to the extent feasible, basic military strategy in a possible general nuclear war should be approached in much the same way that more conventional military operations have been regarded in the past. That is to say, principal military objectives, in the event of a nuclear war stemming from a major attack on the Alliance, should be the destruction of the enemy's military forces, not of his civilian population.
>
> The very strength and nature of the Alliance forces make it possible for us to retain, even in the face of massive surprise attack, sufficient reserve striking power to destroy an enemy society if driven to it. In other words, we are giving a possible opponent the strongest imaginable incentive to refrain from striking our own cities.[3]

And it was acknowledged more explicitly by Mr Schlesinger, a later Secretary of Defense, in 1972. Referring to Mr McNamara's Ann Arbor speech, he said:

> That was in a period of time in which the United States did retain close to a disarming capability against the Soviet Union and recognized it.[4]

After the Ann Arbor speech, the emphasis of public statements shifted back to deterrence and to the discussion of the flexible response in NATO. But in the early 1970s, when the Soviet Union was catching up with the United States and was believed by the United States to possess, or to be on the way to possessing, the ability to knock out the United States' land-based strategic missiles (ICBMs) in a first strike, President Nixon adopted the notion that the United States should aim at 'sufficiency' in the numbers and quality of its nuclear weapons. In his annual messages to Congress, he made it increasingly clear that sufficiency did not mean just an assured destruction capability but a counter-force capability too. A counter-force policy was never spelt out in so many words. Rather, it was put vaguely.

One year the question was posed, 'Should a President, in the event of a nuclear attack, be left with the single option of ordering the mass destruction of enemy civilians, in the face of the certainty that it would be followed by the mass slaughter of Americans? Should the concept of assured destruction be narrowly defined and should it be the only measure of our ability to deter the variety of threats we may face?'[5] Next year that question was answered in the negative in the following terms: 'I must not be – and my successors must not be – limited to the indiscriminate mass destruction of enemy civilians as the sole possible response to challenges. This is especially so when that response involves the likelihood of triggering nuclear attacks on our own population.'[6] In substance that amounts to the old Air Force argument. In 1974, Mr Schlesigner, the Secretary of Defense, stated that a shift from a counter-city to a counter-force policy was proceeding, together with the pursuit of the improved missile accuracies needed for this purpose.[7] And in August 1980, in Presidential Directive 59, President Carter officially endorsed a counter-force strategy. It is doubtful whether the new directive represented a change in policy, rather than a confirmation of a long-established policy, leaked to the press as a step in President Carter's efforts to appear no less tough than Mr Reagan in his election campaign. In the same month, Harold Brown, Secretary of Defense, in a major speech on nuclear strategy said,

At the outset, let me emphasize that P.D. 59 is *not* a new strategic doctrine; it is *not* a radical departure from U.S. strategic policy over the past decade or so. It *is*, in fact, a refinement, a codification of previous statements of our strategic policy. P.D. 59 takes the same essential strategic doctrine, and restates it more clearly, more cogently, in the light of current conditions and current capabilities.[8]

President Carter agreed to programmes for the new missiles and the new control and command systems believed necessary to make the policy feasible.

On the Soviet side, about which there is far less information, we know that they have never distinguished between deterrence and a counter-force strategy and that they have been racing hard with the United States, usually some steps behind: as we saw earlier, they have gone rather ahead in numbers of strategic delivery vehicles but have still to catch up in numbers and refinement of multiple warheads per delivery vehicle. The accuracy of their missiles, which is crucial for a counter-force capability, cannot be known precisely. It has always been held that in accuracy they have been behind the United States, with its more sophisticated and dynamic technological industries, but it is now held, rightly or wrongly, that they have been improving their accuracies to the point where, in combination with their relatively large warheads, they have acquired or are acquiring a first strike capability against ICBMs.

Whether either side will ever really have sufficient confidence in the reliability and accuracy of its missiles to think it can knock out anything like 100 per cent of its opponent's missiles is open to grave doubt. The reliability and accuracy of missiles may be less in practice than tests and theoretical models suggest. The danger is that one side may think the other side is launching a counter-force strike, having fearfully attributed that capability to it, and may retaliate hastily. In June 1980, when the United States had two false though brief nuclear alerts, caused by troubles with a computer system on each occasion about 100 B-52 nuclear-armed bombers were readied for take off – it became clear from the reports of the episode that a 'launch-on-warning' strategy is not a wholly academic notion. It was reported that:

> . . . the Pentagon would have to reconsider the wisdom of moving toward what is known as a launch-on-warning strategy, in which the United States would fire its nuclear forces before any Soviet missiles actually hit American soil. . . .
>
> The administration has not adopted a launch-on-warning policy, but in his annual Defense Department report last January, Mr Brown said that a Soviet surprise nuclear strike was unlikely because "prudent planners" in Moscow could never be sure "that we would not launch our intercontinental ballistic missiles on warning".[9]

The Flexible Response
This second shift in strategy away from deterrence occurred a

considerable time ago but has acquired a new significance as the risks of superpower conflict have shifted from Europe to other parts of the world.

The NATO strategy of the early post-war years was 'massive retaliation', whereby a conventional attack on Western Europe by the Soviet Union would be met by an all-out nuclear attack by the United States on the Soviet Union. This was replaced by the 'flexible response', whereby a Soviet conventional attack on Western Europe would be met, once NATO's conventional forces were in trouble, by using United States nuclear weapons stationed in Europe; United States strategic weapons, the use of which would invite retaliation against the United States, would be kept in reserve.

The development in the 1950s of tactical nuclear weapons, which were quickly introduced into Europe by the United States, created the technical opportunites for the flexible response. The motive for the United States to adopt a doctrine of this kind was present once she believed the Soviet Union had acquired, or was going to acquire, enough long-range nuclear weapons to be able to inflict unacceptable damage on the United States. As Henry Kissinger, who was one of the protagonists of the new policy, put it in 1959: ' . . a nation cannot be counted on to commit suicide in defense of a foreign territory'.[10]

The words in which the policy was formally adopted by NATO were more tactful, tortuous and ambiguous than those of Henry Kissinger. The NATO ministers in their communiqué declared that they had adopted a 'revised strategic concept' and said of it:

> This concept, which adapts NATO's strategy to current political, military, and technological developments, is based upon a flexible and balanced range of appropriate responses, conventional and nuclear, to all levels of aggression or threats of aggression. These responses, subject to appropriate political control, are designed, first to deter aggression and thus preserve peace; but, should aggression unhappily occur, to maintain the security and integrity of the North Atlantic Treaty area within the concept of forward defence.[11]

The main argument adduced in favour of the flexible response is that whereas the Soviets would not believe in, and therefore would not be deterred by, the threat that the United States would use massive retaliation with nuclear weapons in response to a conventional attack on Europe, they would believe the threat that the United States would use nuclear weapons tactically in Europe and that the ensuing nuclear war might then escalate until the Soviet Union was attacked. In other words, it is a more credible deterrent; it increases the uncertainties the Soviets will have to weigh when deciding whether to attack.

The trouble with the flexible response, as Alva Myrdal has argued, is that it turns Europe into a nuclear battlefield where a 'limited nuclear war' might be attempted in the course of a superpower conflict anywhere in the world; it turns the European nations into hostages of the two superpowers:

> Europe is deeply aware of having been selected as a major battlefield if the superpower conflict were brought to a pitch of military confrontation. To the very end these two contending world powers would try to keep each other's homelands as sanctuaries, while Europe would be sacrificed. Weapons are massed in Europe to overkill capacity, targets selected, scenarios set, and buttons ready to be pressed. Year by year, day by day, the perspective of the European nations is one of utter devastation in the event of war, especially in the centre of the continent and the two Germanys.[12]

Thus from the point of view of the nations of Western Europe, the flexible response is not a policy of deterrence in which the European governments, singly or collectively, threaten the Soviet Union with nuclear punishment if she attacks them. Instead, they threaten that in order to stop a Soviet invasion they would have nuclear weapons used by the United States on their own territory. This would be an act of self-immolation without precedent: war games and other analyses have repeatedly shown that limited war of this kind in which 'tactical' nuclear weapons were used would lead to the devastation of Europe with massive civilian casualties.

The notion that this strategy is more credible to the Soviets than the threat of massive retaliation on the Soviet Union by the United States has always seemed to me questionable, unless you assume that the Soviets think it likely that the United States would be ready to act regardless of the wishes of its European allies. For suppose the Europeans alone commanded the tactical weapons in Europe, would they be more willing to start using them to defend Europe, given the devastation that would ensue, than the United States would be willing to start using its strategic weapons against the Soviet Union to defend Europe?

It follows from Henry Kissinger's remark quoted above, that in defence of Western Europe the European members of NATO ought to be more willing to risk the use of nuclear weapons from their territory than the United States would be from her territory that is not directly threatened. So far so good. But we then run into an assymetry: the weapons to be used from European territory are to be used tactically on the battlefield, not pointed at the Soviet Union to deter her.

If Europeans were in charge of them and the weapons technically could be used only on their own territory, or that of the Warsaw Pact members other than the Soviet Union, they might feel that the deterrent threat to the Soviet Union was weak while the risk to themselves was acute. And the Soviets might calculate that this was so. In practice, the deterrent effect of the strategy seems to depend importantly on two beliefs being entertained by the Soviets:

(i) that nuclear war, once started, may rapidly get out of control;
(ii) that the United States, being in command of the tactical weapons in Europe and out of the immediate firing area, might use them regardless of any misgivings of its NATO allies.

Both seem reasonable beliefs. Neither is reassuring.

Europe got itself into this position at a time when the possibilities of conflict seemed greater in Europe than they do now, and when the post-war hesitation about rearming Germany, the divided nation on the East-West frontier, was still very much alive. Moreover the European nations have resisted American pressure to increase their conventional forces and so reduce the dependence of NATO on nuclear weapons to counter the perceived Soviet threat.

The question of who controls the nuclear weapons in Europe, and how, is of vital concern, and is worth exploring further – though the answers one finds are pretty dusty.

Control of weapons

In the Warsaw Pact, whose declared policy is not to be the first to use nuclear weapons, the Soviet Union alone appears to control the nuclear weapons. I know of no provision for consultation within the Pact over the use of nuclear weapons.

In NATO, some United States nuclear weapons are under dual control, i.e. manned by America's allies but with Americans controlling the warheads; others are under single United States control, manned wholly by Americans on United States bases or vessels in Europe.

The notion of a multilateral nuclear force (MLF) under combined political control was once promoted by the United States to assuage an alleged, but apparently fictitious, German appetite for nuclear weapons. But it foundered partly on the difficulties of combined control of nuclear weapons by a series of autonomous states. Similarly the notion of a European nuclear force is floated from time to time by pan-Europeans, but it never takes off because no federal government exists to which member nations would be ready to give the power to release nuclear weapons from their territory. The hostage-like dependence of NATO on the United States has thus occurred because various European members preferred to rely on United States tactical nuclear weapons rather than acquire their own and reject United States weapons, as France has done, or keep nuclear weapons off their territory, as the Scandinavian countries have done.

In order to assuage the feelings of dependence and impotence of her European allies as the doctrine of the flexible response was being adopted by the United States and the motion of a multi-lateral force was being buried, Mr McNamara proposed the creation of a Nuclear Planning Group in NATO. It came into being in 1966. In the words of a review of this body in the official NATO letter, published in 1970:

> NATO's Nuclear Planning Group (NPG) was created in response to a growing desire of the European members to have a greater say in the nuclear policy of the Alliance. The development by both East and West of an invulnerable retaliatory nuclear capability and NATO's shift towards a

69

strategy of flexibility in response made this need more pressing than it was under the conceptionally more simple – but no longer credible – doctrine of massive retaliation. An important incentive was the necessity of taking account of the special position of the Federal Republic of Germany, without giving her – or any other non-nuclear nation – 'a finger on the trigger'. The important German defence effort, as well as the particularly exposed situation of the Federal Republic in the event of war, underlined the desirability for her closer involvement in nuclear planning.[13]

The non-nuclear allies were given a voice in planning for the possible use of nuclear weapons, although most of the weapons themselves remain subject to the control of the United States. It should, perhaps, be stressed that the ultimate responsibility for the decision on the use of the great majority of the nuclear weapons available to NATO, remains with the President of the United States and no military commander may, or can, fire these weapons until after consultation as appropriate and after release of the weapons by the President.[14]

The membership of the group was extended in 1968 and 1969 until it effectively included all members of NATO. It is pretty clear that considerations of secrecy and the very notion of the flexible response means that precise plans for the use of nuclear weapons are not agreed between the United States and its allies in this group.

The main feat of the group was said in 1970 to be agreement on 'political guidelines for the use of tactical nuclear weapons'. This followed the tabling by the United States of 'a paper on the use of tactical weapons as a warning signal' and other papers by other nations. By way of explanation, the 1970 article says:

In contrast to what some press stories suggested at the time, these guidelines are in no way intended to bring about a change of strategy. On the contrary, they constitute an enhancement and explanation of the strategy of flexibility in response, which remains unaltered. The whole question of a possible defensive use of nuclear weapons is approached with considerable circumspection and emphasis is laid on the greatest possible control of the danger of escalation. Thus the guidelines, again contrary to speculation, do not attempt to define the nuclear threshold. This 'threshold' is perhaps more dependent on the stength of conventional forces at the disposal of the Alliance.[15]

Rumours which one heard at the time suggested that the main point which reassured the Europeans was the notion that a warning shot or shots might first be fired on a peripheral target that did not directly invite retaliation on the battlefield. (I have heard an area of Poland mentioned.) These rumours seem consistent with what one can read between the lines of the 1970 exposé cited here.

It is important to note that the Nuclear Planning Group, which for the United States was a means of prolonging United States control and calming its European allies, was sold to the Europeans on the understanding that they would be constantly kept informed of what was happening in any crisis:

> The US Defence Secretary stressed that participation by the allies would only be meaningful if all the interested countries, on the highest political level, could be constantly kept informed about a developing crisis as well as of the factors which could play a role in a possible decision on the use of nuclear weapons.[16]

And it was argued further that one beneficial result of the creation of the Nuclear Planning Group was that:

> The continuous contacts in Brussels at the level of Ambassadors and in the staff-group have enabled the non-nuclear countries to acquire the expertise without which meaningful consultation in times of crisis would be inconceivable.[17]

All this happened in the late 1960s, but I know of no major change in the arrangements or in NATO strategic doctrine since then.

The arrangements adopted were expedients produced to patch up an uneasy relationship. They required trust by Europe in the responsibility of United States leaders.

71

7 Disarmament Diverted

For the 35 years since World War II ended, disarmament talks of one kind or another have continued with few interruptions. A number of treaties have been negotiated and come into force. Yet the arms race has not been checked. The treaties which have been made, though not always valueless, have been peripheral to the arms race: they have been agreed upon precisely because they have not interfered with the arms race; at most, they have redirected it a bit. The strength of the military and the militarist ethos has prevented anything more.

Peripheral measures

After the war, attention at disarmament talks was at first focused on nuclear disarmament and complete conventional disarmament down to the level of forces needed to maintain internal order. In the early 1960s, draft treaties for general and complete disarmament were put down by both the Soviet Union and the United States, but the drafts were not taken up in serious negotiation. Instead attention was turned to 'partial measures'. The pursuit of partial measures was justified by the argument that disarmament was unrealistic or undesirable, that it was better to accept the arms race and try to guide it by the pursuit of 'arms control' – a term coined by strategic theorists which is exceedingly vague but carries the implication that by mutual agreement two nations engaged in an arms race can satisfactorily control the race without going further and seeking to stop it. That is a notion far more satisfactory to the military than disarmament, which puts them out of business.

Between 1963 and 1977, eight main treaties or conventions for partial measures were agreed. These agreements and their characteristics are as follows. I list them in chronological order according to the date they were signed, which is given in brackets.[1]

(a) *The Antarctic Treaty* (December 1959) demilitarizes Antarctica, the long way round between the superpowers. The Arctic, the short way round, is heavily militarized and no restrictions apply to it.

(b) *The Partial Test Ban Treaty* (August 1963) stops testing above ground by the three nuclear parties to the treaty (Soviet Union, United Kingdom and United States) and as such has been a successful anti-pollution measure, even though China and France have continued tests above ground on a modest scale. But it has not stopped nuclear weapons development. More tests have been conducted underground by the superpowers since the ban than were conducted by them above and below ground before it. The figures for numbers of tests above and below ground from 1945 to the end of 1979 are as follows:

	Before	After	Total
	Partial Test Ban		
U.S.A.	293	360	653
U.S.S.R.	164	262	426
U.K.	23	7	30
France	8	78	86
China	–	25	25
India	–	1	1
	488	733	1221

Source: SIPRI Yearbook 1980, p. 364

There is evidence that these public figures for the number of nuclear tests are too low, possibly by a significant margin.[2]

(c) *The Outer Space Treaty* (January 1967) prohibits putting nuclear weapons into orbit. But ballistic missiles (i.e. missiles which follow a ballistic trajectory from the firing point to the target) have so far been more attractive than weapons in orbit; and research and development of vehicles and devices that could be used in space continues.

(d) *The Latin American Nuclear-Free Zone* (February 1967) was established on Latin American initiative to keep out of the arms race a peripheral area where the pressures to admit nuclear weapons, and the possibilities of acquiring them, were relatively slight. Three major countries in the area, Argentina, Brazil and Chile, have either not ratified the treaty or have hedged their positions.

(e) *The Non-Proliferation Treaty* (July 1968) commits non-nuclear states to refrain from acquiring nuclear weapons and nuclear states not to give nuclear weapons to them. In return, the nuclear states, along with all the parties to the treaty, undertook 'to pursue negotiations in good faith on effective measures' relating to the cessation of the nuclear arms race at an early date, to nuclear disarmament and to general and complete disarmament. That was agreed 12 years ago, but the arms race goes on. Most of the nations that really might go nuclear have refused to bind themselves under the treaty: Argentina, Brazil, Egypt, Israel, India, Pakistan and South Africa. In essence, the treaty produced vows of abstinence from the nuclear innocent in exchange for a hollow promise to disarm from the nuclear powers, whilst those experiencing temptation have sat on the sidelines.

(f) *The Sea-Bed Treaty* (February 1971) forbids the fixing of nuclear weapons and other weapons of mass destruction to the ocean floor beyond a 12-mile limit from the shore. It is not clear what this has stopped, since the attraction of the oceans lies in buoyancy and in the possibilities of cheap concealed *movement* that the oceans offer to submarines carrying weapons. It seems like a treaty not to screw aeroplanes to the ground. Presumably anti-submarine weapons – mines or homing torpedoes – might be fixed to the ocean floor, but the problems of maintaining and controlling such weapons while keeping their location secret would seem to be formidable.

(g) *The Biological Weapons Convention* (April 1972) forbids the development, production or stockpiling of microbial or other biological agents in significant quantities and requires the des-truction of existing stockpiles. This is the only true disarmament agreement made so far i.e. an agreement to destroy and forbid possession of an existing type of weapon. Admittedly, biological

74

weapons so far have looked so uncontrollable in their effects on the enemy, and possibly on other populations including the user's, that they have not been very attractive militarily. But a measure which prohibits the possession of weapons produced by a rapidly expanding area of science is important.

(h) *The EnMod Convention* (May 1977) forbids the use of techniques to damage your enemy by changing the environment, meaning 'the deliberate manipulation of natural processes – the dynamics, composition or structure of the Earth, including its biota, lithosphere, hydrosphere, and atmosphere, or of outer space.'[3] In other words, the treaty prohibits some of the wilder forms of futuristic warfare with which the military scientists have flirted, and also herbicidal warfare, which was used on a large scale with grave consequences in Vietnam.

In addition, there have been the SALT (Strategic Arms Limitation Talks) agreements between the Soviet Union and United States and the MBFR (Mutual Balanced Force Reduction) talks between NATO and the Warsaw Pact, and CTB (Comprehensive Test Ban) talks between the Soviet Union, United Kingdom and United States.

In the SALT talks, which were proposed by President Johnson in 1964 and began in Helsinki at the end of 1969, the two superpowers moved out of any wider international arena and took to bilateral, private negotiations over 'strategic' weapons. Britain, which alone amongst lesser powers was in on the negotiation of the Partial Test Ban Treaty, was left out. Under the SALT I agreement, signed in 1972, two steps were taken: anti-ballistic missile (ABM) defences, which looked pretty unpromising, were limited to two sites on each side, later reduced to one site each; and an interim agreement was reached which limited the number of strategic missiles (land-based plus submarine-based) each side might have, but imposed no limit on the number of warheads per missile that could be introduced or on any other 'qualitative' advances that might be made. The SALT II agreement, signed in June 1979 in Vienna by Messrs Brezhnev and Carter, has not been ratified by the United States and its future is uncertain. The agreement limits the number of warheads as well as delivery vehicles (missiles and long-range bombers) to the very high levels indicated in Chapter 3 – 10,000 warheads or more on each side – until 1985, but new generations of strategic missiles can be introduced within agreed limits; and there is so far no check on the race in non-strategic nuclear weapons (i.e. those called 'tactical' or 'theatre' weapons).

There have also been a number of bilateral agreements between the Soviet Union and the United States to do with the regulation of the arms race – the Hot-line Agreement establishing a communications link for use in emergency (1963, updated 1971); the agreement for prevention of incidents on the high seas, including rules of conduct for ships engaged in surveillance of other ships i.e. ships belonging to the other side (1972); the agreement on measures to reduce the risk of outbreak of nuclear war between the two countries, which provides for notification of an accidental or unauthorized firing of a nuclear weapon, notification of detection of unidentified objects, and notification of planned missile launchings beyond national territory (1971).

The Mutual Balanced Force Reduction talks (MBFR), which started in October 1973, have so far produced no results. The two sides have been unable to agree on what would constitute balanced reductions – not surprisingly since geography, weaponry and forces are assymetrical between the two alliances and the notion that Soviet troops in Eastern Europe are in part garrison troops, not frontier troops, needs to be accommodated in the calculation.

The general effect of all these agreements has been to institutionalize the arms race by setting some rules for the way it is run by the two superpowers. Military expenditure goes on unchecked. So does military research and development. The restrictions on the areas where the fruits of research can be applied have been peripheral to the nuclear arms race. Where numbers of weapons have been limited, as in SALT I and II, no substantial reduction has been achieved – except in the case of biological weapons. Instead, figures have been adopted which allow the next round of the arms race, on which the military and their suppliers have their eye, to go ahead, for example the installation of multiple warheads and new generations of missiles under SALT II.

Indeed it can be argued that the SALT agreements have diminished any chances there were for disarmament. Thus Alva Myrdal argues that,

. . . the superpowers have become confined in a cage of their own making. The very fact that their nuclear arms race has been institutionalized in SALT agreements must mean that their freedom of action for any disarming is reduced. They will be even more shackled than before by domestic interests, military, industrial and political, which construe continued arms build-up to match the enemy as an assured right. It will be difficult for critics and opponents to go against what has been firmly institutionalized by bilateral contracts.[4]

The Reasons for Failure

The most visible and direct cause of the failure to achieve greater progress in disarmament can be seen to have been opposition from the military. As usual this is clearest in the United States, where government is open and, as we saw earlier, the Joint Chiefs of Staff are in the habit of giving their views freely to Congress and the public on military matters and also on the international political and economic scene.

In the case of disarmament and arms control, it is necessary for the administration in power in the United States to get the Joint Chiefs of Staff to approve any measures they seek to introduce. Lack of approval of a measure by the Joint Chiefs can be expected to lead to its rejection in Congress. Hence negotiations about disarmament and arms control are as much or more a process of negotiation within the government – where the military, divided into rival services, negotiate with civilians, who in turn are divided into rival government departments – as they are a matter of negotiation between nations. This is true of all countries, but again it is most visible in the United States.

The SALT talks are an interesting example of inter-service rivalry. All the rival military services are represented in the negotiating teams of both sides and one can see that the agreements made so far have been so constructed that they do not oblige the two countries to make any marked change in the balance between strategic weapons operated by rival services, even though a change from vulnerable land-based missiles to submarine-launched missiles would make sense – and is permitted voluntarily. The representatives of the two superpowers from the armed services operating land-based missiles must have felt a common interest in avoiding obligatory reductions in that type of weapon. One wonders whether they, or their colleagues in other matching services, have ever explicitly acknowledged their common interest, in the conference chamber or outside it.

One can cite various examples of how, in order to get through an arms control measure, the military have had to be appeased by compromises or promises which have made a nonsense of the measure. Take the three measures introduced so far which could have had some effect in moderating or arresting the nuclear arms race between the two superpowers – the Partial Test Ban Treaty, SALT I and SALT II.

A comprehensive test ban, outlawing underground as well as above-ground tests, was first proposed in 1954, after the fallout from an American test had hit the crew of a Japanese fishing boat.[5]

There were many years of moves and counter-moves by both sides, including a period for which there was a moratorium on testing. The obstacle, real or contrived, on which negotiations kept foundering was the United States claim that they did not have adequate means of verifying that the treaty was observed and that the Soviets were not secretly conducting underground tests, combined with the Soviet Union's refusal to allow visits by inspectors. Then came the Cuba crisis of October 1962. In the exchange of messages in which Kennedy and Khrushchev settled the crisis, they agreed on the urgent need to reassure the people by making some progress with disarmament and both mentioned a test ban treaty as a promising step. The Soviet Union then made the major concession of offering to permit two or three on-site inspections by foreigners of 'suspicious events' on its territory, to supplement verification by seismic and other monitoring systems positioned outside. They claimed to have been told by the representative of the western powers that three inspections would satisfy them. But the Americans then insisted on eight to ten on-site inspections. A comprehensive test ban treaty was abandoned and the Partial Test Ban, which bans only atmospheric tests, agreed upon.

In order to get the Joint Chiefs of Staff to endorse that agreement and so make possible its passage through Congress, President Kennedy had to agree to four 'safeguards' proposed by the Joint Chiefs of Staff, which made nonsense of the notion that the treaty had anything to do with disarmament or arms control, even though that notion continued to be conveyed to the public. The four safeguards were:

(a) The conduct of comprehensive, aggressive, and continuing underground nuclear test programs designed to add to our knowledge and improve our weapons in all areas of significance to our military posture for the future.

(b) The maintenance of modern nuclear laboratory facilities and programs in theoretical and exploratory nuclear technology which will attract, retain, and insure the continued application of our human scientific resources to these programs on which continued progress in nuclear technology depends.

(c) The maintenance of the facilities and resources necessary to institute, promptly, nuclear tests in the atmosphere should they be deemed essential to our national security or should the treaty or any of its terms be abrogated by the Soviet Union.

(d) The improvement of our capability, within feasible and practical limits, to monitor the terms of the treaty, to detect violations, and to maintain our knowledge of Sino-Soviet nuclear activity, capabilities, and achievements.[6]

Even that was not enough. The Joint Chiefs of Staff laid down 'criteria to insure fulfilment of the safeguards proposed by the Joint Chiefs of Staff with regard to the limited nuclear test ban treaty.' These criteria were sent to the Chairman of the Senate Committee on Armed Services, simultaneously with a statement from the Administration accepting them and saying how they would be met.

As an indication of the commitments the Joint Chiefs of Staff insisted upon, their criteria for the fulfilment of safeguard (a) above were as follows:

(a) The underground test program should be comprehensive. Therefore, it should be revised to include as many as feasible of the objectives of the tests which we would otherwise do under conditions of unrestricted testing.

(b) The underground test program should be vigorous. It should proceed at a pace that will exploit to the fullest the capabilities of existing AEC and DOD weapons laboratories. If these capabilities are proved to be inadequate to meet established requirements, they should be expanded.

(c) The underground test program should be a continuing program designed to insure the highest practicable rate of progress in nuclear technology.

(d) The standards established governing the type and magnitude of tests to be conducted should not be more restrictive than the spirit of the treaty limitations.[7]

In the case of SALT I, under which a ceiling was set on the number of strategic ballistic missiles, but none on their 'quality' (i.e. how many warheads they contain, their accuracy and other characteristics), President Nixon endorsed programmes for more accurate warheads, the new Trident submarine and the B1 bomber. And since SALT I covered only ballistic missiles, the development of the cruise missile was pushed ahead partly as a possible 'bargaining chip' for SALT II.[8] When the President addressed a joint session of Congress on his return from signing the agreement, he used most combative words, presumably in order to quell possible opposition from militarists:

No power on earth is stronger than the United States of America today. None will be stronger than the United States of America in the future. This is the only national defense posture which can ever be acceptable to the United States.[9]

On the other side, we can see from subsequent statistics that the Soviets after SALT I acquired new generations of missiles with multiple warheads in the development and acquisition of which they were far behind the United States. They introduced the SS 20 mobile missile of medium range which is being deployed in Europe and is outside SALT, since it is 'tactical' rather than 'strategic' according to the terminology described in Chapter 3. And on both sides military research and development went on uncurbed.

With SALT II, the military could be seen staking their claims well before the agreement was finalized. Thus in the Posture Statement for the fiscal year 1980, the Chairman of the Joint Chiefs of Staff said,

. . . whatever the outcome of the current round of negotiations on Strategic Arms Limitation, I believe it will be essential to spend more on our strategic forces. The increase need not be as large with an equitable SALT agreement as without, but in either event, we will have to do more in this area. Of particular importance is a commitment to a program for a survivable ICBM[10]

President Carter, before he suspended his request to the Senate to ratify the agreement on account of the Soviet attack on Afghanistan, had committed himself to higher military spending and new programmes to fortify United States nuclear strength within the SALT II ceilings. Two important moves have been the decision to deploy in Europe cruise missiles, which are not covered by SALT but can hit the Soviet Union; and the decision to proceed with the development of the MX system.

The MX (which stand for 'missile experimental') proposal illustrates the heights of technological extravagance to which the nuclear arms race has led and the way in which the technological pursuit of the arms race is diverted, not diminished, by partial measures such as the SALT agreements which limit one avenue of advance – the one down which the military have least desire to go further – and leave others open.

The proposal, which may yet be modified, is for a series of separate loops or 'race tracks' of special roadway, each with 23 bunkers on it at sufficient intervals for no two bunkers to be vulnerable to one Soviet warhead. On each racetrack, there is one missile (ICBM) with ten very accurate warheads. The missile can be moved from one bunker to another by a giant covered vehicle and there left ready for firing, whilst the covered vehicle goes on, moving from time to time around the racetrack, stopping at random at bunkers. By satellite observation, the

Soviets will be unable to tell which bunker contains the missile. But in order to reassure them that there is only one missile on one racetrack, the road leading into the racetrack along which the missile is introduced, which can be observed by satellite, will be visibly blocked, after one missile has been introduced, by a solid bank that cannot readily be removed. In addition, it is proposed that the 23 bunkers on the circle should have concrete lids that can all periodically be removed, one racetrack at a time, so that the Soviets can see by satellite that there is only one missile there. Once the lids are closed after the inspection, the missile is shunted into hiding again.

It is proposed that there should be 200 missiles and racetracks in the deserts of Utah and Nevada, requiring no less than 12,000 miles of new roads. In the summer of 1980, the cost was put at $34 billion.[11] This is the kind of project, however, where the early estimates of costs are often greatly exceeded. Much higher figures have already been suggested.[12] Moreover the technical characteristics of the MX system, and the strategic assumptions on which it is based, have not escaped criticism.[13]

The rationale for the scheme depends on SALT II, since if warhead numbers were not limited, the Soviets might in theory have enough to eliminate all the proposed MX bunkers and have some over.

It is a wildly extravagant system. It appears to owe a lot to inter-service rivalry, for it would be far cheaper to rely on submarine-launched missiles whose location cannot be known precisely, and to scrap land-based ICBMs. That, however, would mean a major transfer of resources from the United States Air Force which operates the ICBMs to the United States Navy which operates the SLBMs. Since the Soviets do not announce their programmes we shall only know how they have reacted in the years ahead when decisions taken now show up in weapons observed by satellite and other means.

In sum, opposition to disarmament from the military and their supporters is clearly visible and is powerful. It is expressed, and no doubt perceived, in terms of duty to ensure that the nation, personified by its military forces, is strong, meaning it can go on keeping up with or ahead of its rival. It is taken for granted that in that way security and peace will be assured.

A second reason why disarmament talks have failed so far to

produce major results is that it is so difficult for two nations once they are locked in an arms race to find intermediate positions between giving up the race altogether (i.e. disarmament) and going on with it full blast. To stop the race means that in both nations the politicians must persuade their constituents that the quarrel which started the race can be forgotten, that the other side can now be trusted, and that it is in the interests of the people in both nations to silence their hawks, disband their military establishments and divert their energies to peaceful aims, meaning the improvement of their respective economies and societies and the diversion of more resources to poor countries. Unless the process is reasonably symmetrical, and seen to be so, the alarmists on one side will be able to claim, convincingly, that the other side is not playing its part, that the nation is at risk, and that disarmament must cease or be reversed. The obvious way to ensure symmetry is by negotiating a complete disarmament treaty, but there are limits, perhaps narrow limits, to how far treaty-making can be a means of creating trust, as distinct from a means of giving expression to that mixture of trust and mistrust which already exists, possibly accentuating the mistrust as bargaining proceeds. Thus to try to negotiate a complete disarmament treaty when mistrust is strong leads to taut bargaining and great difficulties in agreeing on what is a symmetrical programme for arms reduction, and what is an acceptable method of verifying compliance with the treaty.

On the other hand, if partial measures, rather than complete disarmament, are pursued, one is attempting to regulate a race the very rationale of which is distrust and the pursuit of relative strength. That would be bound to be fraught with difficulties, even if everything was symmetrical: if there were, say, two powers with identical armouries and symmetrical geography. In practice, alliances, armouries and geography are not symmetrical. One superpower has more weapons in one category or is more advanced in one dimension of weaponry, the other side has advantages elsewhere. One has a geographical advantage of one kind, the other another. Hence to attempt to limit one kind of weapon, or dimension of a weapon, to an equal number on both sides – be that number zero or something larger – may be to upset the overall balance between the two sides. Yet to agree on anything but equality is very difficult. To do so implies that you can agree on a calculation of the overall balance of power within which you can assess the relative value to each side of the item in question and that the balance in the remaining items will remain roughly as it is and will not be upset by changes made in reaction to the limitation of the selected type of weapon. Further, it implies that when the resulting unbalanced limit for a particular item is agreed and presented for ratification, the politicians on the side which accepted the lower figure can defend themselves successfully against their hawks, who will inevitably argue that inferiority in the item in question is dangerous and a sign of weakness.

It is perhaps surprising that disarmament talks have kept going for so long when the difficulties look so great. But one can see some patterns of behaviour which help to explain the apparent contradiction between an arms race which shows no sign of slowing down and disarmament talks which go on almost without interruption:

(a) If you look at the leaders of the superpowers, their behaviour seems contradictory, but one element in their behaviour seems to be a desire not to be remembered only as leaders who took part in the arms race, endorsing military requests for more arms without doing anything to stop the race. Kennedy is associated with the Partial Test Ban; Johnson tried hard to start SALT before the end of his term; Nixon produced the SALT I agreement and agreed to give up biological weapons; Carter tried, until Afghanistan, to deliver a SALT II agreement. On leaving office, United States presidents have cried out about the dangers of the arms race. The Soviet leaders express similar views. In making gestures against the arms race like this the leaders are presumably expressing their own feelings of concern, which are probably accentuated by the daily burden of being responsible for 'the button' and by their detailed knowledge of arms and the arms race. They are presumably also responding in some degree to public opinion.

(b) The Soviet Union and United States are almost continuously engaged in a dialogue about disarmament and arms control either bilaterally through the SALT negotiations, or through the inter-alliance negotiations between NATO and the Warsaw Pact over mutual balanced force reductions in Europe, or multilaterally through the Committee on Disarmament in Geneva, which meets sporadically but is never disbanded, like the talks between the rival powers in George Orwell's *1984*. While the agreements they have made have done little or nothing to stop or slow down the nuclear arms race, each side from time to time publicly makes a proposal for a substantial arms cut, only to be accused by the other side of hypocrisy on the grounds, for example, that it is engaging in propaganda, attempting to divert attention from some wickedness in which it is alleged to be engaged, or making a proposal that is heavily biased to its advantage, any or all of which accusations may be true. It can be argued that the result is to preserve the *status quo,* including superpower nuclear dominance over other countries: the superpowers go on racing and so, besides perpetuating a deadlocked race between themselves, they achieve huge nuclear supremacy over third countries, whose pursuit of nuclear weapons they restrain by engaging with them in disarmament and arms control talks. This does not imply that disarmament talks are part of a Machiavellian design by the superpowers, only that the forces operating within and between nations may have produced the situation described. This interpretation rests on the questionable assumption that the possession and accumulation of nuclear weapons, even if unused, sustains or increases the power of the superpowers. That is an issue to which we shall return in Chapter 9.

(c) Amongst the different countries, those who push nuclear disarmament most strongly are the non-aligned nations and some of the smaller nations which belong to NATO and the Warsaw Pact, for example Canada, the Netherlands and Poland. The superpowers play them along in negotiations over partial measures, such as a comprehensive test ban or the outlawing of the production and stock-piling of chemical weapons (the use of which is already outlawed), whilst conducting SALT negotiations privately elsewhere. The way the game is played and the feelings of the non-aligned nations about it are excellently set out in Alva Myrdal's book *The Game of Disarmament.*[14] The increasing frustration of the non-aligned and non-nuclear countries was forcefully expressed at the 1980 conference to review the Non-Proliferation Treaty, where many non-aligned countries united in denouncing the superpowers for failing to fulfil their promise to start disarming – the promise they made in 1968 in exchange for promises from non-nuclear nations to renounce nuclear weapons.[15]

(d) The second-rank nuclear powers (second-rank in terms of nuclear forces) occupy an ambivalent position at the disarmament table. They are excluded by the superpowers from the top-rank negotiations. They do not like the indignity of joining the 'weak' and running with the non-aligned and other non-nuclear nations in pursuit of disarmament. So you would expect to find them keeping away from the game or on the edge of it. And that, broadly speaking, is where they have been. France was very active with Britain in pushing for disarmament when, under Khrushchev and Eisenhower, there seemed hope in the mid-'50s that real progress might be made with disarmament in negotiations where France and Britain enjoyed a formal status no different from the superpowers. But when de Gaulle came to power, France held aloof from disarmament talks, taking the position that when the superpowers disarmed, which they showed no sign of doing, she would join in willingly. China for a long time was excluded from the talks but her position was similar to that of France.

Britain has been a semi-detached appendage of the United States. Sometimes she has adopted a common position with the United States, claiming privately to have influenced that position for the better. At other times Britain has put up independent proposals publicly and tried to draw the United States towards them. But since the mid-'50s, those proposals have never been radical.

Part Three

British Policy,
Past and Proposed

8 Britain in the Nuclear Arms Race

History

The story of why and how Britain got the bomb has been superbly told in the official history by Margaret Gowing, whose work I have drawn upon freely in what follows. She also covers, as a minor theme, the story of how Britain admitted United States nuclear weapons to bases here and then sought to have a say in their use.

It is a story of the ambivalent behaviour of a sinking power linked to a stronger one, wanting but failing to be treated as an equal partner, alternating between the pursuit of independence and the willing acceptance of dependence.

Following the discovery of the results of splitting an atom of uranium in 1939, the year of the outbreak of World War II, scientists in many countries questioned whether an atomic bomb was possible, but scientific explanations seemed to encourage scepticism. It was the Report of the British Maud Committee[1] composed of scientists (including refugees), which in 1941 showed lucidly and with great cogency how and why an atomic bomb was possible and that the Germans might already be working on one. As a direct result of this Report the desultory American project was expanded into what became the huge Manhattan project. Britain's conception of herself as a nuclear power was born out of this early work of her scientists. Because the United States had far greater resources – the cost of making the first bombs was colossal – and America was safe from bombing and invasion, the United States became the dominant partner in the enterprise, and the development and production of the bomb were undertaken in the United States.

From the beginning, co-operation had its ups and downs. In 1941 and 1942 there was close co-operation. Then the United States severed connections for nine months. They were restored on Churchill's insistence in a formal agreement made at Quebec in August 1943, which said *inter alia* that neither country would use the bomb against a third country except by mutual consent, nor give information to third parties without mutual consent; that post-war industrial or commercial benefits would be shared on terms specified by the United States President (a clause which was never effective); and that they would jointly allocate uranium of which they, together with Canada, had achieved command of supplies in the allied world.[2] After the Quebec Agreement, most of the British atomic scientists went to the United States and Canada to work on the bomb.

It was not clear how long the different clauses of the Quebec Agreement were to last, but the uncertainties seemed to be cleared in September 1944 when Roosevelt and Churchill signed an aide-memoire which said that the full collaboration in the development of atomic energy for military and civil uses should continue until terminated by joint agreement.[3] However, Roosevelt died within six months and no other American knew of the existence of the agreement until told by the British.

On 6 and 9 August 1945, bombs were dropped on Hiroshima and Nagasaki. Britain's status as a junior partner was apparent: the decision was essentially American, although the British Government's consent was duly asked for and duly given by Churchill.[4]

At the end of July the Labour Party had come to power in Britain. No member of the new government, not even Mr Attlee, the deputy Prime Minister in the war-time coalition government, had been admitted to knowledge of the atomic bomb by Churchill. As an interim measure Mr Attlee adopted the extraordinary procedure, suggested by the Secretary of the Cabinet, of retaining Sir John Anderson, who had been in charge of atomic matters under Churchill, to handle them for the new Government (which he opposed on most matters from the Opposition front bench). He continued for a time under Attlee, reporting directly to him on matters where ministerial decisions were called for.

At the end of the war British scientists who had worked in the United States knew a great deal about the fabrication of bombs and also a good deal about the production of one of the two fissile materials – uranium 235. No British scientists had worked in the large-scale United States plants which made plutonium, the other fissile material which was to be the ingredient of Britain's first bomb. However, the Anglo-Canadian team in Montreal had worked on a pilot reactor and pilot plutonium separation plant.

In November 1945, in the afterglow of the war, there was agreement between Truman and Attlee for continued atomic co-operation, loosely and briefly defined. But the Americans reneged on this, except for a deal over the one issue where the United States wanted something from Britain, rather than the opposite. This was the question of how to share uranium supplies. The United States was the main consumer of uranium, but Britain still held control over supplies via the Commonwealth and via her position as a partner with the United States in an agreement made in 1944 to buy all the uranium output of the Belgian Congo.

At the end of the war the United States required legislation for the domestic control of atomic energy. The McMahon Bill provided what the scientists had fought for – a civilian rather than a military Atomic Energy Commission – and as such was seen by Americans as a great liberal Act. But in order to preserve the so-called 'secret' of the bomb, especially in the wake of the exposure of the Canadian spy ring and the passing of information to the Russians by Dr Nunn May, a British physicist, severe restrictions were imposed on the dissemination to foreign countries of 'restricted data'. This comprised information not only about the manufacture or use of atomic weapons and the production of fissile material but also about its use for power production. To most of the British, the Act passed in 1946 seemed not just a betrayal of the wartime partnership and promises, but a disaster because they believed that American technological collaboration was essential to their project. In practice this collaboration would have been useful but was not essential for building atomic plants and a primitive bomb. It was, however, of the greatest political and strategic concern to Britain and was to be important in the technology of more advanced atomic weapons. For these reasons, as well as wider questions of status and Anglo-American relations, it became a prime concern of British governments, whether Labour or Conservative, to get these McMahon restrictions lifted.

A British decision to produce fissile material had been taken before the McMahon Act was passed, and there was from the outset a general assumption in all atomic quarters that Britain was going to make atomic weapons. But the absence of any provision for research into bomb fabrication revealed that no specific decision to make a bomb had been taken.

In January 1947 the small group of British ministers who dealt with nuclear policy decided, without reference to the full Cabinet, to go ahead and produce the weapon in the utmost secrecy. They were advised by a very small group of civil servants, scientific advisers and military men. Professor Gowing summarizes the reasons for the decision as follows:

The British decision to make an atomic bomb had 'emerged' from a body of general assumptions. It had not been a response to an immediate military threat but rather something fundamentalist and almost instinctive – a feeling that Britain must possess so climacteric a weapon in order to deter an atomically armed enemy, a feeling that Britain as a great power must acquire all major new weapons, a feeling that atomic weapons were a manifestation of the scientific and technological superiority on which Britain's strength, so deficient if measured in sheer numbers of men, must depend. A bomb would not be ready in any case for five years, so that the decision was of the variety that was impossible *not* to take rather than of the type that must be taken for urgent and immediate purposes.[5]

Later in 1947 '. . . when it was suggested that Britain might rely on the United States for the maintenance of her nuclear striking force, Lord Tedder, Chief of the Air Staff, voiced a general feeling when he replied that this would involve a close military alliance with the United States in which Britain would be merely a temporary advance base, would involve complete subservience to United States policy and would render Britain completely impotent in negotiations with Russia or any other nation.'[6] The mood at that time was for a partnership of equals, not dependence.

The first public intimation of the decision to make the bomb came only in May, 1948. In an answer to a Parliamentary question, the Minister of Defence said, '. . . research and development continue to receive the highest priority in the defence field, and all types of weapons, including atomic weapons, are being developed.[7]

Since 1947 a great deal has changed:

(a) NATO was formed in 1949 and for more than 30 years the United States has been committed to join in the defence of Western Europe. During that period she has acquired huge economic interests in Europe.

(b) The frontier between NATO and the Warsaw Pact and the frontiers of the neutral countries between them – Finland, Sweden, Austria, Yugoslavia – have come to be accepted, and a dialogue has been established between the Soviet Union and the United States, and between the alliances, in which they alternately bark and negotiate over a variety of matters.

(c) Britain's economic position has deteriorated dramatically relative to her Continental neighbours, in particular Germany. She is now the poor relation in the European family.

(d) Britain's important military commitments outside Europe, which were the legacy of empire, have gone – with trivial exceptions.

(e) Britain tested its first bomb (a fission device) in October 1952 and its first hydrogen bomb (a thermo-nuclear device) in 1957, having enjoyed little American co-operation in the meantime. But once Britain had successfully discovered the secrets of nuclear weapons, the Americans saw the advantage in sharing information again. So in 1958 the Americans passed, and in 1959 amended, an agreement for Co-operation on the Uses of Atomic Energy for Mutual Defence Purposes between the two countries. The result of this was that Britain was put in a special position, above that of America's other allies, for purposes of sharing knowledge about nuclear technology, in particular about how to make warheads, but also about other matters such as how to make the nuclear reactors to propel submarines.[8] There ensued a period of quite close co-operation, followed by renewed restraint on the American side in the latter half of the 1960s as

93

Britain shuffled towards Europe and there was reference to the possibility of a European nuclear force or co-operation with the French as a way of softening their apparent Anglophobia.[9]

(f) Britain managed to produce a first generation of long-range delivery vehicles, the V bombers which could reach Russia, but abandoned the attempt to produce a ballistic missile (Blue Streak) with American help, to replace the V bombers. Instead, Britain turned to the United States, and after the abortive attempt to get Skybolt (which was cancelled by the Americans) eventually obtained Polaris missiles under the Nassau Agreement of 1962 between Kennedy and Macmillan. There has been no subsequent attempt to make long-range missiles in Britain.

(g) Britain's capacity to design and produce warheads has been maintained at the cost of spending, without prior Parliamentary approval, a sum estimated in January 1980 at £1,000 million, on producing a British system of multiple warheads to help penetrate the Soviet anti-ballistic missile defences of Moscow,[10] even though the installation of such defences by the Soviet Union is narrowly circumscribed by the SALT I agreement of 1972.

(h) It is now planned that Britain's four Polaris submarines should be replaced by four or five submarines carrying Trident missiles supplied by the United States, with British-made warheads, an arrangement similar to the one under which Polaris was obtained. The cost, including the submarines, which will be built here, is now put at £5,000 million at 1980 prices, a huge figure which may well be exceeded. The new submarines will not begin to come into operation until 1992 and the spending will be spread over many years.

(i) Two conditions which explicitly or implicitly have helped persuade the United States to supply us with long-range missiles and other forms of help with nuclear weapons are, firstly, that all our nuclear weapons, including the V bombers and other weapons we have produced ourselves, have been assigned to NATO; and, secondly, that we have provided the United States with bases in Britain for nuclear weapons and for many other military activities.

Before considering an alternative policy for Britain, there are four questions to examine:

(i) In what sense, if any, are Britain's long-range nuclear weapons independent, given that they are largely supplied by America and are assigned to NATO?

(ii) Have any better arguments than those offered by the Government been given for Britain's trying to possess independent nuclear weapons, and if so what is the strength of those arguments?

(iii) What control does Britain have over American nuclear weapons in Britain?

(iv) What is the extent and nature of United States bases in Britain?

Independence
It is useful to distinguish three kinds of dependence, two technical and one political.

1. *Long-run Technical Dependence*
Britain has been dependent on the United States for Polaris missiles, designs and know-how for nuclear-powered submarines, tritium (a form of hydrogen used in making hydrogen bombs), intelligence information about targets, precise mapping of the Soviet Union and other matters. These are things that are incorporated in a British Polaris submarine or are on board when it sets out on patrol. By deciding to withhold these things the United States could not stop a submarine out on patrol from firing its missiles. But it presumably could cause Britain's force of Polaris submarines to become increasingly unserviceable for lack of spares for the American-made missiles and related systems, unless alternative arrangements could be made. In that sense Britain's Polaris force may be technically dependent on the United States in the long run. The same will be true of the proposed Trident force, though tritium will now be produced in Britain.

95

2. *Short-run Technical Dependence*

Since the invulnerability of Polaris submarines depends on their staying under water, they need a signal system that permits them to receive orders while submerged and a navigation system with which they can fix their position precisely while submerged: a ballistic missile can be directed accurately at a remote target only if the starting point is known precisely. Dependence on the United States for these facilities would have great significance, for it could mean that the United States could prevent us firing our missiles or reduce our ability to do so safely and accurately.

There is, understandably, rather little information on this subject. What I have been able to find is this:

(a) *Communication:* it seems to be well established that very low frequency radio is used to communicate with submerged submarines, since at this frequency radio waves will penetrate the water. Britain has transmitters at Rugby and Criggion. In nuclear war, communication at very low frequency may be disrupted through damage to the ionosphere, which reflects the waves back to earth. Hence alternative systems must be provided. How far Britain relies on the United States for communication systems of either kind or shares systems with the United States is not known. But she clearly could have independent systems for normal use or as a fallback, possibly at the price of greater vulnerability through having fewer transmitters or needing to come nearer to or above the surface to a greater degree than would be the case with shared facilities.

(b) *Navigation:* for very precise position-fixing the Americans have a satellite system, Transit, from which a submarine can position itself from a coded reading if it raises an antenna to the surface for ten minutes or more,[11] and a land-based system, Loran C, from which a submarine can position itself with a submerged antenna. Britain has no similar navigation systems of its own, but its submarines carry Transit and Loran C, making use of American transmissions. Technically, it would be simple for the Americans to scramble their Transit and Loran C transmissions and deny them to all but United States users. However, British submarines also carry other navigational aids, including Omega and Decca and inertial guidance systems.[12]

The conclusion seems to be the same for navigation as for communication: Britain may use American facilities normally but it probably can act independently of them, possibly at some cost in accuracy or vulnerability – or should be able to do so if the possibility of independent action has been planned for.

3. Political Dependence

The formal position is that our force of V bombers is assigned to SACEUR, the American supreme commander of NATO's forces in Europe, whereas our Polaris force is more loosely assigned to NATO. Both forces get their targets from the United States strategic planners, though Britain has a say in the choice.[13] In the event of war, the plan appears to be that the Nuclear Planning Group would be consulted before nuclear weapons were used in a 'flexible response'; and if the point came where SACEUR wished to call on Britain's V bombers, he would ask the British Prime Minister to authorize their use. In the case of the Polaris force, it is less clear where the initiative for use might come from. When Macmillan made the deal with Kennedy under which Britain obtained Polaris,

> It was stated that 'these British forces will be used for the purposes of international defence of the Western Alliance in all circumstances'. However Macmillan ensured the insertion of a crucial qualifier: 'except where Her Majesty's Government may decide that supreme national interests are at stake'.[14]

Thus there is a political commitment, subject to a qualifier, not to act independently. That commitment does not look like an insincere or reluctantly given promise, since it fits the policy that Britain has followed with little variation since the war, of seeking and emphasizing co-operation with the United States and accepting dependence on her, a policy for which the rock-bottom argument has been that it will help to keep the United States involved in the defence of Europe.

To sum up, Britain's present long-range nuclear forces appear to enjoy short-run technical independence; but in the medium term they may be technically dependent on the United States;

97

and politically they are committed, subject to a qualifier, to NATO, meaning essentially that the United States, consulting Britain, plans their use, and Britain decides whether to execute the plans. It is a curious role to be played, voluntarily, by one of America's poorer allies which is suffering a progressive economic decline.

Rationales

Lawrence Freedman, in his excellent review of British nuclear policy, to which reference has been made, ends by surveying the rationales offered for Britain's policy of possessing an 'independent' nuclear force. He does not question the underlying assumptions that there is a Soviet threat in Europe and that the risk of nuclear war is worth incurring. Rather he implicitly accepts the assumptions of official policy and analyzes it on its own ground in a mood of avowed agnosticism. Having noted that official statements are rare, brief and unchanging, he sets out the following as the main rationales on offer:

(a) *The second centre of decision-making*: this is the argument that (i) in a crisis the Soviets might mistakenly think the Americans, having lost their resolution, wouldn't use nuclear weapons and (ii) in those circumstances the thought that Britain, a second nuclear power, might use hers, would deter the Soviets from whatever they were thinking of doing. As Freedman points out, a second centre may hinder not help NATO's power to make decisions; but, more important, it is difficult to see why Britain should ever want to start a nuclear war when others hesitate, nor why her action in so doing should draw the United States to use its nuclear weapons, rather than just bring down Soviet nuclear weapons on Britain – a view also put by Field Marshal Lord Carver, a former Chief of the Defence Staff.[15]

(b) *The contribution to NATO*: Freedman notes that Britain's NATO allies have never shown any enthusiasm for the contribution of independent nuclear forces by Britain and France, contributions which may increase reliance on nuclear weapons relative to conventional weapons, and may permit their owners, Britain and France, to opt out of a war – though in Britain's case the importance of American bases on her soil probably prevents a withdrawal to safety.

(c) *The 'insurance policy'* against the United States failing in a crisis to live up to its nuclear guarantee or balking away from that guarantee in the long run. This policy will be effective only in so far as medium-term technical dependence on the United States, and any short-run dependence, can be circumvented. Again it is as difficult to visualize the circumstances in which Britain would want to act independently as it is under (a) above – the 'second centre of decision-making' argument.

(d) *The political argument:* nuclear weapons bring influence. Britain's recent history of rapidly declining influence scarcely supports this argument. And Freedman only goes so far as to say that a nuclear arsenal still demands some sort of respect and 'in circumstances difficult to predict, it might be the most valuable source of international power',[16] a statement which seems to mean that he cannot think of any circumstances in which a nuclear arsenal would be a valuable source of power.

Freedman's conclusion is that Britain has nuclear weapons, and is likely to go on having them, for no better reason than inertia:

The politics of beginning or terminating some activity are usually far more difficult and complicated than the politics of carrying on as before. To add or subtract a nuclear capability would command attention: to maintain it would barely be noticed. This is why it seems likely that Britain will continue to be a nuclear power well into the next century.[17]

This conclusion is consistent with the conclusion we reached at the end of Part I: that Britain would have no grounds for acquiring nuclear weapons now.

The common thread one can see in Margaret Gowing's history of how Britain acquired nuclear weapons, and Freedman's review of why Britain goes on with them, is the folly of a declining power which seeks influence on the one hand by ingratiating itself with the United States and becoming dependent on her and, on the other hand, by buying and maintaining nuclear symbols of independence from the United States, symbols for which it has no use since it does not seek to be independent. A by-product of the policy was that Britain ruptured her war-time bonds over nuclear matters with Canada and France, a policy which, far from preventing France obtaining nuclear weapons, encouraged her to do so on her own.[18]

Control of United States Bases

British control – though that is perhaps too strong a term to use – over the use of the United States nuclear bombers now in Britain, and of the cruise missiles that are planned to be stationed here, seems extraordinarily informal.

It seems clear that the cruise missiles, like the nuclear bombers that use British bases now, will not be subject to 'dual key' control, whereby a member of the British as well as American armed forces has technical control of firing. That system applies to those American tactical nuclear weapons on the Continent, of which the delivery vehicles are manned and, as a rule, paid for, by a European host nation, while the warheads are looked after and owned by the Americans. It applied to the Thor missiles which were based in Britain 20 years ago.

There is only political control, meaning agreement by the United States to ask the British Government before using nuclear weapons from Britain.

In the debate on nuclear weapons in the House of Commons on 24 January 1980, various members asked about control. The main thrust of the replies given by Mr Pym, then Secretary of State for Defence, was to keep the Opposition quiet by referring in vague terms to agreements which had been in operation under both Labour and Conservative Governments. The cruise missiles 'are to be owned and operated by the United States within the long-established framework of the agreements between our countries; agreements which cover any use of United Kingdom bases in war . . .'[19] When asked if the British Prime Minister had a veto over American actions, Mr Pym replied that use of the bases would be 'a matter of joint decision' by the two Governments. 'It is a long-established convention that has, I believe,

100

survived for many years under Governments of both parties.'[20]
And Mr Hayhoe, a junior defence minister who wound up the
debate for the Government, made clear that the relevant
agreement with the United States dates back to the early 1950s:

The arrangements are precisely those that we have had for
nearly 30 years during which time they have always covered
bases in the United Kingdom from which aircraft such as the
B47 and F111 have been able to reach the Soviet Union. There
is nothing new or mysterious in any of this.[21]

To see what Mr Hayhoe was referring to, we can turn again to
Margaret Gowing's official history. The story is amazing and
goes right back to the Quebec Agreement, under which both
countries had to consent to the use of the bomb by either.

At the meeting in November 1945 between Truman, Attlee
and the Canadian Prime Minister, Mackenzie King, two of their
advisers, Sir John Anderson of Britain and General Groves,
director of the United States Manhattan Project, jointly proposed a list of points to be incorporated in a document to replace
fully the wartime Quebec Agreement. The first point was that
the three governments would not use atomic weapons against
other parties without prior *consultation* with each other. This was
a significant dilution of the Quebec Agreement. 'Consultation'
was used in place of 'consent'.[22] But this document came to
nothing. In the United States there were political obstacles to it
being turned into either a secret agreement or a public one.
Moreover there was 'something of a furore' when in May 1947 a
committee of Congress had been told about the 'consent' clause
in the Quebec Agreement.[23] The subject therefore lapsed.

By 1948, the Cold War had begun, the Marshall Plan had been
launched, and the main aim of British foreign policy was to rally
its continental neighbours and to ensure that America was
committed to the defence of Western Europe. Against this
background there were two important developments.

In January 1948, in an effort to restore some element of the
atomic partnership which had been severed by the McMahon
Act, Britain negotiated a *modus vivendi* with the United States.
This finally buried the wartime Quebec Agreement. The United
States agreed to restore some exchanges of technical informa-

tion, while Britain, in return, surrendered important claims to supplies of uranium in favour of the United States, which urgently needed larger supplies. Britain also agreed to give up the claim that the United States, before using the bomb, had to seek British consent (the Quebec formula) or consult with Britain (the abortive Attlee-Truman formula of 1945). 'Most curiously, in view of the potential issues of life and death that were involved, neither officials nor Ministers showed any concern or interest in the surrender of Britain's veto, or right to consultation on the use of the bomb.'[24] They were intent upon the restoration of co-operation, but the technical co-operation achieved 'in the event turned out to be extremely limited'.[25]

The second major development came in the middle of the year. In June 1948, as the Berlin blockade and airlift began, Britain, meaning Mr Attlee and three other ministers, agreed to an American request to station some strategic bombers in Britain. They did this so quickly and unreservedly that the Americans are reported to have been taken by surprise.[26] No written conditions were laid down concerning the circumstances in which the bombers might be used. The bombers were brought in during the emergency created by the Berlin blockade, and were not, at first, equipped to carry nuclear weapons, but they were allowed to stay permanently, and in time were equipped to carry nuclear weapons.[27]

It has been reported that at the military level preparations for the stationing of American bombers in Britain had been under way since 1946, the year the last United States Air Force unit left Britain after the war. An 'informal' agreement was apparently made between General Carl Spaatz, commander of the United States Strategic Air Forces in Europe and Air Marshal Tedder, 'whereby five East Anglian RAF bases would be prepared to handle B-29s if required'.[28]

The realization that Britain had no control over the possible use by the United States of its nuclear weapons in Britain began to worry Bevin, the Foreign Secretary. There was discussion with the Americans in 1950, in response to which the United States ambassador confirmed in a letter Britain's right to terminate the arrangement to base American bombers here but said nothing about consultation or consent before the bombers were used – though that issue had been raised by the British. British officials recognized the importance of control over use, but there were fears that a letter to the Americans on the subject 'might cause suspicion and offence'.[29] The issue was put to ministers who decided that nothing should be done 'on the grounds that in practice this issue could hardly arise unless British policies had diverged so far from those of the United States that American use of the airfields would have to be reconsidered anyway'.[30]

This supine position, taken in secrecy, was later reversed. There appear to have been two reasons for this, both connected with Truman's reference at a press conference to the possible use of nuclear weapons in Korea. After Attlee rushed to America to dissuade Truman from thinking of using the bomb, the statement he made to the House of Commons was cast in such vague terms that Churchill discovered for the first time that the Labour Government had not held on to the clause on the use of the bomb in the Quebec Agreement – an agreement he had made and the existence of which was still a secret. He was incensed.

Secondly, the promise Truman made to Attlee at this time about consultation over the use of the bomb was not written down and was soon repudiated; and the British Chiefs of Staff, having seen in the case of Korea how the United States might at short notice think about the use of nuclear weapons, and recognizing that on a future occasion they might want to make use of British bases, took the view that the present arrangements were inadequate. Their reaction was ambitious. They sought to get agreement with the United States about their general plans for the use of nuclear weapons; they sought partnership in nuclear planning and did so by pleading that it was intolerable not to know in what circumstances Britain might be put at risk. The Americans stone-walled and pleaded the political difficulties of accepting any constraint on their freedom to use atomic weapons.

Eventually, in October 1951, a solution was reached by Oliver Franks, then British Ambassador to Washington. He, in Margaret Gowing's words, was 'anxious to avoid a situation where the question of the Americans using their British bases to launch atomic attack became a sudden political issue' and persuaded the Americans to agree to a statement which concluded with the formula that the question of the use of the air bases and facilities in the United Kingdom in an emergency 'naturally remains a matter for joint decision in the light of the circumstances at the time'.[31] The American National Security Council agreed that these words could be used if required but understood the British would not use them unless they needed to. The gist of the formula was given to the House of Commons by Churchill in December 1951, a few months after he became Prime Minister again.[32] When he visited the United States in January 1952, the Americans repeated that British bases would not be used without British consent. In the communiqué published after the conference the Americans put their names to that assurance publicly for the first, and so far as I can find, the only time.[33] The words used were these:

> Under arrangements made for the common defence, the United States has the use of certain bases in the United Kingdom. We reaffirm the understanding that the use of these bases in an emergency would be a matter for joint decision by H M Government and the U S Government in the light of the circumstances prevailing at the time.[34]

That appears to be the assurance to which ministers still refer.

The reluctance of the Americans to make public declarations about limitations on their freedom to use foreign bases is understandable. They presumably have two main aims: to convey to the Soviet Union that they are unfettered; and to sustain their bargaining position with the many nations where they have bases of different kinds by limiting the knowledge each has of the terms agreed to by others.

The Extent of United States Bases

American military bases in Britain are astonishingly numerous and serve a great variety of purposes. Britain's strategic position explains why the Americans, given the opportunity, have so many bases here. As an offshore island, Britain is relatively safe from invasion. Bases and depôts here are therefore unlikely to be captured; she is close to the sea routes along which shipping brings supplies to northern Europe and along which Soviet submarines must pass on their way from the northern Russian bases to the Atlantic; and she is a good staging post for American troops and supplies being transported to the Continent.

104

Until recently there was little information readily available to the public on American bases in Britain. The British authorities released little or no information. A lot of information was available from American sources and specialist journals, but nobody pieced it together. Parliament and the public have shown little interest in the subject and the strategic analysts seem to have averted their eyes from it.

During the summer of 1980, however, persistent questioning of the Defence Minister elicited first a list of 12 bases, comprizing major air bases and Holy Loch (the American Polaris base), then a list of 53 bases and finally, in a third round, a list of 56 bases which was said to include all those previously omitted.[35]

Recently Duncan Campbell, that remarkable investigative journalist, has published a brilliant analysis in which he lists 103 bases and facilities;[36] and a major report on foreign bases in many countries, including Britain, is nearing completion at SIPRI.

From the cross-checking I have been able to do with information available from SIPRI and other bits of evidence, Campbell's analysis appears to be accurate. Of course there may be errors and omissions, but the general picture he gives seems to be right. He uses a wide definition of 'bases and facilities'. For example, he includes intelligence and communication facilities; facilities operated by civilian agencies (the CIA and United States Coastguard Service); and facilities operated with British participation. And he includes bases held in reserve for use in emergency by the United States forces.

Campbell's map is reproduced as Figure 1. His main findings are these:

(a) 'In Britain, the US forces have at least 21 air-bases used or reserved for them, 9 transportation terminals, 17 weapon dumps and stores, 7 nuclear weapons stores, 38 communications facilities, 10 intelligence bases, and 3 radar and sonar surveillance sites. Of these, the majority clearly contribute at least as much to strategic global "US only" options as to the options for defending Europe.'

Fig 1: Duncan Campbell's map of American bases and facilities in Britain

Source: New Statesman 31 October 1980

Fig 2: Soviet map of British and American bases in Britain

Source: Great Britain; Geographical Conditions, State System, Economy, Elements of Infrastructure, *Foreign Military Review,* May, 1980

(b) In an article on Britain in a Soviet military journal, a Soviet officer, Colonel Leskov, recently described how 'The Pentagon maintains a ramified network of bases, stores of nuclear and conventional weapons, headquarters, communications centres, intelligence centres and other installations.' Clearly drawing on intelligence data, Leskov listed nuclear weapons stores and provided an astonishing map of Britain with dozens of key locations and air bases marked or mentioned. The map, on which both British and American bases are marked, is reproduced as Figure 2.

(c) The United States has installed a network of communications bases in Britain so that its communications within Britain and abroad can be independent of the Post Office and the British military communications system.

(d) It keeps a huge base in South Wales and another in Shetland at the end of chains of sonar devices for monitoring Soviet submarines, whose nuclear missiles are likely to be aimed at the United States, not Europe. This is cited as an instance of how Britain, through having bases here, risks pre-emptive attack for the sake of the defence of the United States.

(e) Campbell provides a remarkably rich list of spy bases, ranging from the permanent stationing of spy 'planes of various kinds in Britain to the presence of major listening posts for monitoring Soviet radio traffic and for tapping international telephone traffic from Britain and other countries, as well as various bases for communicating with intelligence and communication satellites.

From this evidence it seems pretty clear that the Americans have enjoyed an open invitation to do what they like in this country, and, understandably, have taken advantage of it. They have penetrated the country like woodworm getting into a piece of old furniture.

Just as the legitimacy of the American bases for nuclear bombers and missiles is obscure, so too is that for other varieties of base. For example, there have been stories recently that the possibility of moving American nerve gas supplies into Britain has been under consideration, an idea reportedly favoured by some British 'hawks'. Who would decide whether to take such a step? Would Parliament be consulted, or even informed?

The presence of so many American facilities here has two important implications:

(a) To remove the whole lot would be felt, rightly or wrongly, to be a major upheaval. How far it would really affect the international situation is a subject to which we shall return. But in the official world the notion has been held without question that it is obviously in our interests to have the Americans here, and that to ask them to go would not only be an act of folly but would scarcely be feasible. As an official once put it to me, 'We are tied to the Americans as Gulliver was tied to the ground, with hundreds of little strings; it would take a superhuman effort to break all the strings.' The contrary view that we have become an American aircraft carrier, loaded with weapons and likely to be blown up in any war in which the United States becomes involved, no longer seems to worry officials or the military, though, as we have seen, it was a prospect which did worry Lord Tedder and his colleagues in 1947, when the decision to produce a British bomb was made.

(b) To keep out cruise missiles or remove American nuclear aircraft based here would still leave a large number of American targets in Britain against which Soviet nuclear weapons are likely to be aimed.

Secrecy and Democracy

Whatever one may think about Britain's policies towards nuclear weapons and American bases described here, it is impossible not to be shocked and alarmed at the way they have been decided upon and executed without the prior consent of Parliament, and without the public being informed.

The main facts are these:

(a) Churchill created the precedent of excluding most Cabinet ministers, as well as Parliament, from discussion of atomic weapons during the war, but the practice has continued ever since. Decisions are made by a small group of ministers operating in an ad hoc committee or a small regular committee with a meaningless code name, for example the prefix GEN or MISC followed by a number. This committee is understudied and advised, like all ministerial committees, by a committee of officials. Typically, the committee consists of the Prime Minister,

Minister of Defence, Foreign Secretary and Chancellor of the Exchequer, but the composition has varied according to the way responsibility for atomic matters has been divided between departments and according to the talents of individuals. For example, a minister without portfolio may belong, or the Home Secretary if civil defence is in vogue.

(b) Spending on the development of nuclear weapons has been concealed from Parliament and the public. In Margaret Gowing's words,

> When Mr Churchill returned to 10 Downing Street, he was surprised and impressed by the size of the atomic energy project built up by the Labour Government. He found with a mixture of admiration, envy and the shock of a good parliamentarian that his predecessors had spent nearly £100 million on it without informing Parliament. He felt he would have been branded as a warmonger for a similar feat, and one of his early minutes on his return to office was to ask the Permanent Secretary of the Treasury how this very large sum had been hidden away in the accounts. Nevertheless, he maintained the same policy, albeit with a qualm.[37]

Recently, expenditure of £1,000 million on Chevaline, the multiple warhead developed by Britain for her Polaris missiles, was concealed, 'making it the largest matter in recent years not to have gained a passing mention in the annual defence estimates.'[38]

(c) The practice seems to have been that the acquisition and cost of delivery systems – the V bombers, Blue Streak, Polaris and now Trident – are made public. Indeed it would be difficult to keep them secret, since they involve major orders to the aerospace and ship-building industries here or in America. On the other hand, the acquisition and cost of warheads is kept secret. It is understandable that there is secrecy about warhead technology and that government establishments which make the warheads should be under wraps. One does not want everyone to know how to make bombs. But that does not mean that the amount of expenditure on warheads need be kept secret. Nor does it mean that, as happened with Chevaline, secrecy should be extended

110

from the design of the warhead, meaning the design of the fissile materials and trigger mechanisms which produce the nuclear explosion, to the fact that the third stage of the missile is being re-designed so that it will eject multiple re-entry vehicles which go in different directions, some containing decoys, in order to penetrate anti-missile defences. Here one is dealing with part of the delivery system and with the kind of decision – whether or not to acquire multiple warheads – which is usually debated openly and at length in the United States. Moreover in this instance secrecy has shrouded spending that is of questionable value. As noted earlier, the installation of anti-missile defences by the Soviet Union was narrowly circumscribed by the SALT I agreement.

(d) Parliament as a whole has failed to display any significant interest in nuclear weapons. In the whole life of the Labour Government from 1945 to 1951 there was not one debate in the Commons on atomic energy, military or civil, only occasional references to the subject in connection with foreign affairs or defence, which were, paradoxically, hotly debated.[39] The debate in the Commons in January 1980, during which the plan to acquire Trident was announced, was the first debate on nuclear weapons for 15 years.[40] How many debates there were between 1951 and 1965, I have not established. Amongst members of Parliament there has of course been a small minority who have voiced their opposition to nuclear weapons at question time and other times; and there has been a similar minority who have taken a militant pro-nuclear position. But that is about all.

(e) Labour Governments have been at least as guilty as Conservative Governments of concealing their decisions and hushing up the subject of nuclear weapons policy.

The pursuit of secrecy and avoidance of public debate about British nuclear weapons cannot be justified, since the early days of nuclear weapons, by the need to keep our policies a secret from the Soviet Union. In the United States, nuclear policy, and the acquisition of new weapons or devices comparable to Chevaline are, with rare exception, debated openly in great detail. And the Soviet map of Britain suggests, as one would expect, that the

111

Soviets have long ago undertaken for themselves the exercise now being done by Duncan Campbell and SIPRI and have pieced together the evidence available on American bases from open sources in America and here – as well as which they will have had evidence from reconnaissance satellites, from American radio traffic which they have monitored, and from other intelligence sources.

In practice, secrecy and the autocratic handling of nuclear policy have served to keep the British public and Parliament ignorant. Nor is that an accident. It is clear from the histories of British nuclear policy that ministers and officials have sought to keep the subject out of politics. In that way they have fostered 'The tradition of secret and bipartisan policy-making with its emphasis on continuity . . .'[41] It is also clear that, at least in the early years of which we have an official history, it was ministers, not officials, who were primarily responsible for the extreme pursuit of secrecy.[42]

It is not surprising that the decision-makers, starting with ministers, should be content to govern in secret rather than in public. Secrecy means that your decisions and advice, about which you may have doubts, are not exposed to criticism – at least not until many years later, by which time you will have moved on to another job, retired or died. Secrecy, by limiting the number of people engaged in making a decision, means that the decision-makers privy to the secret feel that they belong to an inner circle, a super-élite. And with military matters, and nuclear weapons in particular, the need to act in secret can be perceived as a patriotic duty or even as a wider duty, since the fate of mankind may be affected. Moreover, if the Prime Minister and his senior colleagues demand secrecy – and leaders of the Opposition have done so too when they have been in office – it may be hard for officials to resist ministers, though they surely should do so when it comes to concealing from Parliament the use to which money voted by Parliament is put. That practice has plainly become scandalously excessive.

But the motives for secrecy of the inner group of ministers who have taken the nuclear decisions do not apply to the outer group of ministers who constitute the large majority of the Cabinet, nor to Parliament. At first sight it is extraordinary that these excluded groups should have been resigned for so long to being kept in the dark and should still apparently be in that mood.

112

The possible reasons seem to be these:

(a) Cabinet ministers and Members of Parliament, like many members of the public, may often be reluctant to think about nuclear weapons and the American bases that are associated in their minds with them. These are nasty subjects. As a Cabinet minister or Member of Parliament, the more you engage in debate about them, ask for information and demand to have your say, the more you will share responsibility for policy. Consciously or unconsciously, you may prefer to avoid that responsibility.

(b) Criticism of British nuclear weapons policy and American bases and curiosity about them have come to be associated with the left wing of the Labour Party. To be critical of a policy or to challenge the practice of secrecy is to risk being labelled as someone who is soft on the Soviets, anti-American or a soft-headed idealist, certainly not a reliable man. Some of the most violent criticism comes from the right wing of the Labour Party, using 'unilateralist' as a vulgar term of abuse. This stream of criticism may have the effect of inhibiting people in all parties.

(c) Precisely because opposition to British nuclear policy comes from the Left and has periodically divided the Labour Party, Labour governments, wishing to avoid rows and to keep their actions secret from their flock, have probably been worse about secrecy than Conservative governments. Between 1945 and 1951 they first hid peacetime expenditure on nuclear weapons from Parliament and the public, and they quietly allowed American bases to be established in peacetime, without any public debate. In 1974, they secretly took the final decision to go ahead with Chevaline.[43] Conservative governments, which have been broadly united on nuclear policy, have publicized their decisions to procure major new weapons systems – Polaris in 1962 and Trident in 1980 – though the fact that these decisions, which could scarcely have been kept quiet, were made during a period of Tory government may have been an accident. Broadly speaking, Conservative governments have carried on the bi-partisan practice of secrecy.

(d) Inertia and continuity must be partly to blame. Once the practice of secrecy is established, it becomes a habit; and it is hard to change to openness without revealing what you have been hiding previously and being 'found out'.

(e) Finally, there is the power of the party leader who decides, when in power, whom he will select as a minister and whom he will promote to the best ministerial positions. Those members who are a nuisance over nuclear affairs and secrecy will not improve their chances of being looked on with favour.

None of these is a respectable reason for secrecy. Nuclear policy is a matter of supreme importance. It is a scandal that it has not been debated openly with the benefit of the maximum amount of information consistent with the preservation of really important military secrets.

And it is deplorable that Parliament has allowed its power to control expenditure, hard won in battles with arrogant monarchs, to be abrogated by a handful of ministers using the device of secrecy.

9 The Setting

In Part I it was concluded that, starting from scratch, there would be no case for Britain to acquire nuclear weapons, or let in United States bases. Britain would be safer without them.

Before examining what alternative policy Britain might pursue, we need to see what we can say about the present and future value of nuclear weapons; and we need to make some assumptions about the future.

The Utility of Nuclear Weapons

I shall eschew American-style strategic theory, which rests on the assumption that 'rational' nations are consistently aggressive and are constrained only by the threat of nuclear punishment, not by any political constraints. I shall try to see what lessons, if any, can be drawn from history since 1945.

First, what are the constraints which help prevent any enemy attacking you with conventional and nuclear weapons, respectively, if you do not possess nuclear weapons? Second, how are those constraints upon your enemy, and his incentive to attack you, changed if you possess nuclear weapons? Thirdly, how are the constraints and incentives changed if you have the nuclear forces of an ally based on your territory?

Without Nuclear Weapons

Since 1945 there have been many wars fought with conventional weapons in many parts of the world. International law and the United Nations Charter have not been closely respected. The political opprobrium suffered by nations which attack one another has sometimes been loud – for example Vietnam and Afghanistan – but it has not been very effective. The political constraints on conventional war have been weak.

On the other hand, there is the striking fact that when nuclear

115

nations have fought non-nuclear nations, as they have done quite often, they have never used nuclear weapons since Hiroshima and Nagasaki were annihilated in 1945.

Consider the contrast between Japan, where the United States used nuclear weapons, and Korea and Vietnam where the United States considered doing so but refrained. These are all cases of a nuclear power using or considering the use of nuclear weapons against a non-nuclear power in order to win a war being fought on the territory of the latter.

We can presume that in Korea and Vietnam the expected political costs of using nuclear weapons were deemed to outweigh the expected military benefits, and that the political costs in the minds of the decision-makers were a mixture of the adverse effect on East-West tension and the arms race, the opposition of America's allies to such a course of action, and the burden of guilt and possible unpopularity that the President and American government would have to carry subsequently. But why did not these considerations prevent the use of nuclear weapons against Japan? The obvious answer is that the use of nuclear weapons for the first time was different. Nobody knew quite what would happen. The nuclear arms race had not begun. The public had no opinion about nuclear weapons. The cult of nuclear deterrence, according to which the use of weapons is a disaster but the accumulation of them in order to threaten disaster is desirable, had not been born. Nor had opposition to nuclear weapons, which also emphasizes that their use would be a disaster.

Fear of retaliation by another nuclear power does not appear to have been the reason why the nuclear powers have not used nuclear weapons against a *non-nuclear* country since 1945. I know of no evidence that this was why the United States did not use or threaten to use nuclear weapons against Korea or Vietnam; nor that this was why Britain did not use them against Egypt in 1956; or France against Algeria; or China against Vietnam in 1979; or the Soviet Union against Afghanistan in 1980. Rather, the reason seems to lie in the political constraint. Another cause must have been the limited utility of nuclear weapons for winning a war, in the sense of defeating your enemy's forces so as to acquire his territory and win over or dominate his people, rather than exterminate them.

116

Consider now the hypothetical case of a nuclear nation which, being invaded and overrun by a non-nuclear nation or nations, uses nuclear weapons as a desperate measure to halt the enemy and defend its homeland. Israel and South Africa are probably in this category. Both nations appear furtively to have acquired nuclear weapons, or at least the ingredients for them. It is not incredible that they might use those weapons to defend themselves: the political cost to the white South Africans or Israelis of being overrun, and probably slaughtered or expelled from the territory they now hold, would be so great in the eyes of their governments that the political costs of using nuclear weapons might seem worthwhile. Admittedly, these are special cases. In both countries, there are local peoples, the Arabs and Africans, who challenge the claim of the ruling people to the territory; the ruling people may fear for their lives, and they may also have unusually callous feelings for their potential enemies, the Arabs and Africans, regarding them as members of inferior species. Bitter conflicts generate feelings of that kind.

Nevertheless the distinction between the first category (Japan, Korea, Vietnam) and the second (Israel and South Africa) suggests a hypothesis which, if correct, would be important.

Hypothesis 1: Since the world first witnessed the effects of nuclear weapons in Japan, the political objections to their use have been sufficiently strong relative to the military advantages for a nuclear power not to find it to its advantage to use nuclear weapons against a non-nuclear power – though it might do so *in extremis* to defend its own homeland.

To try to see how strong or weak the political constraint has been, we can look at the evidence to see whether threats of nuclear attack have been made against non-nuclear nations. How close has the political constraint come to being breached?

There are difficulties of definition. A nuclear threat can range from a public statement, 'If your government does not do x, we shall attack your forces or cities with nuclear weapons', to the quiet deployment of nuclear-armed aircraft, ships or other weapons in a manner calculated to be seen by the other side as a warning move.

The information publicly available must be assumed to be

117

imperfect. The following are the results of the limited search that I have been able to make:

(a) There appear to have been no instances of open public nuclear threats being made against non-nuclear nations, let alone yielded to, unless one counts the wild and vague threat to Britain, France and Israel (of whom only Britain possessed nuclear weapons at the time) made by the Soviet Union in 1956 when the invasion of Egypt by those three countries was being brought to a halt anyway.

(b) According to Truman's memoirs,[1] his public reference in November 1950 to the possible use of nuclear weapons in Korea, which caused Attlee to hurry to Washington, was not a calculated threat; he said at a press conference that the United States 'will take whatever steps are necessary to meet the military situation . . .' and was drawn by reporters into saying that he included 'every weapon that we have' and then into saying that 'There has always been active consideration of its use' (meaning the atomic bomb). In a 'clarifying statement' issued the same day, it was emphasized that there was no change in policy and that 'Consideration of the use of any weapon is always implicit in the very possession of that weapon.' What the episode primarily suggests is that at that time the United States was more ready to think and talk about the use of nuclear weapons than were Britain and other countries.

(c) The Cuban missile crisis is in a different category, having been between two nuclear powers. And so is Dien Bien Phu, when the provision of some nuclear weapons was proposed to the French by the Americans but was not taken up.

(d) There is one case where it has been authoritatively claimed that a threat of use of nuclear weapons was made privately – and with success. That is Eisenhower's claim that in order to get a settlement in the stalemated armistice negotiations in Korea in 1953, the Americans 'dropped the word, discreetly' in India, in the Formosa Straits area and at the truce negotiations that, in the absence of satisfactory progress, the Americans 'intended to move decisively without inhibition in our use of weapons, and would no longer be responsible for confining hostilities to the Korean Peninsula.' 'Soon,' he says, 'the prospects for the armistice negotiations seemed to improve.'[2]

(e) Nuclear weapons were deployed twice in defence of the offshore islands in the China-Taiwan conflict before China had nuclear weapons.

(f) A Brookings Institution study[3] lists 19 incidents in which United States strategic nuclear forces were used to make a threat, defined as a 'nuclear signal', between 1946 and 1973. But apart from episodes we have mentioned already – and excluding three odd episodes where bombers were used to 'reassure US allies', two of them in Latin America – these were mostly moves by the United States *vis-à-vis* the Soviet Union after she had acquired nuclear weapons. Commonly, strategic bombers were moved closer to the Soviet frontier or were put on alert. The study concludes, with reference to threats mostly made against the Soviet Union and some against China, that 'the United States has used nuclear threats sparingly; moreover, their use was more common in earlier years – when the U.S. strategic position *vis-à-vis* the Soviet Union was dominant – than more recently.'[4]

(g) It has been claimed that a nuclear threat or threats were made against North Vietnam by Nixon,[5] but the evidence so far is not very convincing. If threats were made, it is not clear what, if anything, they achieved.

(h) Finally, one would expect that if threats had been numerous we would have heard more about them, for one would expect the victims, sometimes at least, to publicize secretly-made threats so as to arouse public opinion and enlist the support of governments in condemning the threatener.

If correct, the evidence that threats against non-nuclear powers have been few supports the hypothesis that the political constraint on calculated nuclear attacks against non-nuclear nations has been strong. So does the evidence that in so far as threats have been made, they have been furtive. Indeed a second hypothesis follows from the first and seems consistent with the evidence.

119

Hypothesis 2: In a world where the political constraint is strong, a public threat by a nuclear power to use nuclear weapons against a non-nuclear power, except in defence of its homeland, will be likely to rebound to the disadvantage of the threatener; and for that very reason it will probably not be a credible threat.

The implication of the two hypotheses is that, since a non-nuclear nation has had little reason to fear nuclear attack or threats of nuclear attack, it has had little incentive to acquire nuclear weapons unless it has felt threatened by *conventional* attack and it has been unable or unwilling to raise sufficient conventional forces, including actual and prospective help from allies, to be confident of holding off that attack. Even then it will have needed to consider whether it was worth incurring the risks of engaging in a nuclear arms race with its enemies.

Recently, for example, Israel, faced by the prospect that nuclear weapons may be acquired by some of her Arab neighbours, who do not all display moderation, has been indicating interest in a Middle East nuclear-free zone. The reports imply that she might be ready to renounce nuclear weapons if her neighbours would do so too.

These hypotheses may help to explain why more nations have not acquired nuclear weapons.

With nuclear weapons

Consider now how your security as a nation is changed if you acquire nuclear weapons.

You may feel you have increased your defences against conventional attack or have maintained them on the cheap – in so far as nuclear weapons are cheaper than conventional forces. But there are the risks of entering the nuclear arms race to be set against that. These are of two kinds. By acquiring nuclear weapons you may weaken the political constraint which prevents nuclear powers attacking you or threatening you with nuclear weapons. For if you join the nuclear 'gang', you may reduce the moral and political support you will get from the community of nations if you are threatened by another nuclear power. No one should forget how in the Cuban missile crisis the United States and Soviet Union confronted one another with nuclear weapons and aroused horror and fear around the world. Condemnation of one party or the other took second place. Secondly, you may provoke your enemy to acquire nuclear weapons, if he does not already possess them; you will expose yourself to the risk that your enemy will make a pre-emptive strike against your weapons, if he fears an attack by you; and you will expose yourself to the risk that misunderstanding or simple errors will lead to weapons being fired during a confrontation or at any time. These, as we have seen, are risks which have been increasing as accurate weapons capable of hitting one another have been developed, and as doctrines have been evolved for fighting nuclear wars with those weapons. They are risks which will increase as the number of nuclear weapons increases.

With foreign bases

The effect of admitting to your territory foreign nuclear weapons will be the same as that of acquiring your own nuclear weapons, except in so far as control is exercised by the foreign power rather than you, and its interests and actions can be expected to differ from yours. Similarly, your enemy's policy will be influenced by what he perceives to be the difference between control by you and control by your ally of weapons on your territory.

Assuming that your ally alone controls the nuclear weapons, the difference compared with controlling them yourself would appear to be as follows:

(a) You can maintain more conventional forces, other things being equal, insofar as your ally, rather than you, pays for the nuclear weapons on your territory.

(b) Your ally may be more or less cautious than you would be about using nuclear weapons to defend your territory, and he may use them in a way which ensures that you, not he, is hurt.

(c) Your enemy as well as your ally may prefer to settle on your territory, rather than in direct nuclear exchanges between their homelands, disputes to which you are not a direct party. This risk will depend on the frequency and intensity of those disputes relative to those in which you are directly involved for the sake of your national security.

The importance of the political constraint

So long as the political constraint holds and can be expected to hold, non-nuclear countries need not fear calculated nuclear attack or threats of nuclear attack from nuclear powers, and they have little incentive to acquire nuclear weapons. Conversely, the possession of nuclear weapons gives their owners no direct power to bully other nations: it is their convential forces which do that.

That is not to say that nuclear weapons have always been valueless to their owners. They may have served to deter conventional attack upon nations which could not or would not raise sufficient conventional forces to deter their enemy, and which failed to settle their differences with their potential enemies by political means. But that limited defensive function, requiring few weapons, is unlikely to be sustainable. Either there must be a political settlement and agreement to dispense with nuclear arms – or to limit them so narrowly that they might as well be dispensed with – or an arms race is likely to ensue, with fear breeding weapons and weapons breeding fear. That is what has happened between the two main nuclear powers. The accumulation of nuclear weapons to match nuclear weapons and nuclear weapons to destroy nuclear weapons in tens of thousands must be reckoned not just valueless, but insanely dangerous. The potential devastation that may be wrought if a nuclear war starts bears no relationship to the risks of conventional war or the political issues at stake.

The main risk of war probably comes from the risk of accident and misunderstanding, combined with unwillingness to lose face. But the political constraint may be weakened if the arms race, and the militarization of society which goes with it, causes politicians seeking office to compete with one another in the toughness of their military policies; or if weapons spread to more bellicose countries.

If the political constraint were swept away by nuclear attack, or threats of attack, by present or future nuclear powers, we would be in the world of the nuclear strategists. Only fear of nuclear punishment would prevent nuclear nations attacking others, or threatening to do so. The argument for nuclear proliferation would be compelling. How else could nations deter their enemies? In the ensuing proliferation of arms races, there would be a high likelihood of nuclear wars.

Moreover the nuclear power or powers who initially broke the constraint would not find their military power enhanced by their actions – except in so far as they had destroyed other countries. For they would have moved from a position where the value of their weapons as a means of imposing their will on other nations was nullified by the political constraint to a position where it was progressively nullified by the deterrent effect of nuclear weapons in the hands of all nations which could make or buy them. To use or threaten to use nuclear weapons is to provoke proliferation of nuclear weapons to other countries; and to do that is to counter-balance your own weapons. Nuclear weapons should not be over-valued. Nor should the importance of the political constraint and its preservation be under-valued.

Trends

To formulate British policy it is necessary to make a few assumptions about trends in the world. I shall adopt the following:-

(a) The arms race between the Soviet Union and the United States continues, possibly subject to arms control agreements. The race does not slow down.

(b) The Soviet Union and United States continue to compete for influence in the Third World, using civil trade and aid, military trade and aid, subversion and, from time to time, military support. The Soviet Union will regard their actions as legitimate because they are helping local socialist political movements and helping political changes which they perceive to be inevitable and desirable. The United States will regard their actions as legitimate because they are helping anti-socialist political forces, and are seeking to prevent political changes which they perceive to be avoidable and undesirable. It is not clear that the politico-economic system and the militarized patterns of aid offered by either the Soviet Union or the United States are well suited to the

Third World countries, let alone that Third World countries whom they pull over to their side will be loyal to them or stick to them for long. But the likelihood that the Soviet Union and United States will fail as imperial powers cannot be relied upon to prevent them competing with one another and using their huge military forces in competitive ventures.

(c) The opportunities for nuclear proliferation will be increasing all the time with the advance in education and technological levels of developing countries and the spread of the ability to make fissile material. The political constraint may prevent countries acquiring nuclear weapons. But the opportunity to acquire them will spread and in some countries the political constraint may be weak. That may be no direct threat to Britain, but the risks of nuclear war in, say, the Middle East may increase.

10 An alternative policy

We turn now to an alternative policy for Britain starting from the fact that it possesses nuclear weapons and is full of American bases.

This means considering military policy and disarmament policy together: they are two sides of the same coin. And it means considering both unilateral policy and multilateral policy towards disarmament (and armament). In other words, it means considering both those policies pursued independently and those pursued in concert with other nations after negotiation of a treaty or understanding.

The notion that unilateral and multilateral policies for disarmament are mutually exclusive is surprisingly common. It is the result of internal feuds within the Labour Party in which the terms 'unilateralist' and 'multilateralist' have been used vulgarly as slogans by rival factions. It is clearly nonsense. While pursuing multilateral measures of disarmament, the achievement of which depends on the agreement of other countries, it is necessary to decide what level of arms to maintain; and that means you need to have a unilateral policy towards the single coin called armament if you look at it one way and disarmament the other.

The criterion set out in Chapter 1 will be used, namely how far policy makes the prospects of peace in Britain better or worse for ourselves and our grandchildren, due consideration being given to the effect of British policy on the fate of other countries.

A criterion we shall discount is how far alternative policies contribute to the pursuit of British influence. The pursuit of influence is put forward sometimes as an argument in favour of acquiring nuclear arms, sometimes as an argument for getting rid of them. These are arguments that need to be treated with great caution, if not contempt.

Often the politicians, officials, journalists and others who advocate that Britain should adopt a given policy for the sake of international influence – the prime examples have been member-

ship of the Common Market and possession of nuclear weapons –
fail to distinguish between the interests of the British people and
their personal interest in being at or around the top table.

The idea that Britain, by possessing nuclear weapons, has
acquired 'influence' may have had some validity in the late 1950s
and early 1960s *vis-à-vis* the United States, but it has become
increasingly hollow since then. Britain's nuclear weapons, as we
have seen, are scarcely independent of the United States. Britain
is not invited to the SALT talks, which are the top table for
nuclear powers. The story that the British Government is glad to
stay away from SALT, lest limits be put on the number of her
nuclear weapons,[1] smacks of sour grapes. The truth is that
Britain's influence has sunk with the failure of its economic
performance, compared with Germany, Japan and other countries. That failure may have been due partly to Britain's high
ratio of military spending to national output and, in particular, its
high spending on military research and development, part of
which has been devoted to nuclear weapons.

It is important to be consistent. The decline in Britain's
influence in the world applies to its capacity to influence other
countries by proposing or taking steps towards disarmament, just
as it applies to its capacity to influence other countries by the
possession of arms.

This has two implications. It means that those who advocate
multilateral disarmament and nothing else are effectively saying
that Britain should take no action until other countries, over
whom we have little influence, make up their minds to act. And it
means that those who advocate unilateral disarmament by
Britain cannot assume that other countries will be strongly
influenced to follow Britain's example – or to react in the
opposite way, for example by acquiring nuclear arms to replace
those abandoned by Britain. Probably Britain's strongest potential card in bargaining is that it can offer or withhold strategically
desirable bases.

Military Policy
The policy to be considered in the light of the analysis in Part I is
the renunciation of Britain's nuclear weapons, which is mainly a
problem of getting rid of a status symbol, and the removal of

United States bases and facilities in Britain. This raises three main questions:

(i) Whether to leave NATO, bring home British troops from Germany and go neutral.

(ii) Whether, if Britain stays in NATO, to remove all United States bases and facilities from Britain.

(iii) Whether to increase, decrease or change the composition of Britain's conventional forces if the American bases and British nuclear weapons are removed.

The argument for going the whole hog, leaving NATO, removing all American bases and facilities and becoming neutral is that it would be an unqualified gesture of confidence in the defensive position of the Soviet Union in Europe and of rejection, not only of nuclear weapons, but also of an alliance with nuclear powers.

The objections to leaving NATO are, firstly, that it would mean renouncing at a stroke a pact, made amongst nations whose values we share, to go to the help of one another. Secondly, it would mean taking a very large step, instead of moving more gradually so as not to upset our allies in NATO nor suggest to the Soviets that there is no willingness on our part jointly to defend Western values. Thirdly, it might make the Warsaw Pact countries and the West Germans more jumpy by increasing, at a step, West Germany's responsibility for its own defence.

For these reasons, I favour staying in NATO. And I favour keeping troops in Germany for the time being if, as is to be expected, Germany wants them there. It is for consideration whether Britain should keep those troops assigned to NATO or follow the French in assuming more autonomy over the troops, subject to contingency plans to commit them to NATO.

The possibilities with American bases and facilities are:

(i) to remove the lot, subject to taking over any facilities whose maintenance is in British interests, and perhaps subject also to having contingency plans to admit American weapons and forces at our discretion in emergency;

(ii) to remove 'nuclear' bases, if they could be satisfactorily defined; or

(iii) merely to insist on 'dual-key' control of all nuclear weapons in Britain, so that Britain technically has control of a safety catch.

127

In this case I favour the first course, since I believe a major move of this order is needed to detach ourselves from the United States and reduce the possibility that we might be the victim of nuclear attack as a consequence of her adventures in other parts of the world. In this respect, I would like to see our sovereignty restored in a *Gaulliste* manner.

To the extent that money was saved on the development, acquisition and manning of nuclear weapons, more could be spent on conventional weapons with no increase in the military budget. In so far as any facilities now paid for and run by the Americans were taken over, that would be a new claim on the military budget.

Whether more or less should be spent on conventional forces depends on your assessment of the Soviet threat, as well as your assessment of the conventional balance. My own belief, as indicated in Chapter 2, is that there is no need to spend more.

The conclusion that in Europe and elsewhere there should be greater reliance on conventional weapons and less on nuclear weapons is one which many others have reached. It has often been urged by the Americans. But that has been within an orthodox framework in which it is assumed that the Warsaw Pact is eager to invade Western Europe and that any change from nuclear to conventional forces should be only a matter of degree, a move which would make the doctrine of the flexible response less dangerous by increasing the chances that it would be possible to defend Western Europe without resort to nuclear weapons. In arguments of that kind there has been no challenge to the notion that there is a Soviet military threat to Western Europe, nor a suggestion that nuclear weapons should be removed completely.

The way to introduce the policy proposed here would be for Britain to explain to its NATO allies, as the French did in a memorandum in March 1966, that the nature of the threats to peace had changed since NATO was formed in the early post-war years and that Britain was changing her policy accordingly. The threat that the Soviet Union would invade Western Europe had diminished. The threat from the nuclear arms race between the Soviet Union and United States had increased. Britain had therefore decided to remove US bases and renounce its nuclear weapons. Britain would stand by the North Atlantic Alliance. It would keep its conventional forces stationed in Germany. It would allow time for American bases and facilities to be removed from Britain in an orderly way.[2]

The French action led to an orderly, if expensive and tiresome, redeployment of American forces and NATO infrastructure, including the removal of NATO Headquarters from France to Belgium. The alliance remained intact. With French routes gone, NATO's established supply lines became more restricted and concentrated on the Low Countries and Britain. The loss of American bases in Britain would restrict the supply lines and staging posts through which to move reinforcements into Europe, though the extent of the loss would depend on what contingency plans were made, to be implemented at British discretion. The object after all is not to dismantle the alliance but to reject nuclear weapons and restore British autonomy over military facilities on its territory; to return to a normal peacetime alliance, in place of an arrangement whereby Britain surrenders autonomy to a superior ally in a manner appropriate only to war, acute emergency or colonial status.

Disarmament Policy

I start from the position that the ultimate aim of policy must be international nuclear disarmament. Unless the nuclear arms race is stopped and reversed, the occurrence of nuclear war, or wars, is probably just a matter of time. Quite possibly it will occur within the lives of our children and grandchildren.

On the other hand, I recognize that the Soviet Union and United States show no signs of agreeing on nuclear disarmament. They are racing hard with each other, whilst they argue about arms control.

What then can Britain do to foster nuclear disarmament?

In the international forums where disarmament and arms control are discussed, Britain and other nations face a dilemma. If they advocate radical disarmament, they risk being called unrealistic and getting no immediate response from the Soviet Union and United States. If they advocate small partial measures, on the grounds that they are more realistic, they may generate activity, in the shape of negotiations often with no outcome; but they risk perpetuating the arms race by endorsing

129

the assumptions on which it rests, namely, that balance in each of many categories of weapons matters; that the owners of nuclear weapons have political differences that justify their huge armouries; that the Soviet Union and United States really are 'superpowers', endowed, like comic-strip heroes, with extraordinary potency through the size of their nuclear armouries. In short, to engage in discussion of partial measures is to perform an act of obeisance to the 'superpowers' and their nuclear armouries.

Present British policy, as noted in Chapter 8, is to follow the latter course, advocating partial measures that are known, or thought likely to be, acceptable to the United States.

I have come to the view that this policy is not merely useless but counterproductive too. In the first place, such agreements as have been made have been largely cosmetic: as we have seen in Chapter 7, they have served to give an impression of order and progress towards disarmament where there is none; they have been a means by which politicians, consciously or unconsciously, have lulled public opinion and eased their consciences. Secondly, if a particular type of weapon is selected as a subject for negotiation whilst the need to engage in the arms race goes unchallenged, the result can be that the military embrace that weapon more closely into their armouries than they would otherwise have done.[3]

The alternative is to base policy on the view that the Soviet Union and United States are clumsy dinosaurs which are losing their economic and political potency as they dissipate their resources in a perilous arms race, that they are animals best mocked and isolated, not pleaded with and asked to agree some Queensberry Rules[4] of nuclear sport.

The implication is that Britain should change its policy to advocacy of radical nuclear disarmament, meaning the rapid reduction of nuclear arsenals by steps, and nothing less.

Since there is such huge overkill, the steps need not be very evenly balanced and could be taken unilaterally, in part at least. An agreement to adopt the old proposal of a 'minimum deterrent' whereby both sides would pause, each with a handful of invulnerable strategic weapons in, say, submarines, might help to reassure the two sides that a balance would be kept once the level of weapons was so low that relative numbers might begin to matter.

Unless the Soviet Union and United States both come to see the futility and danger of their nuclear arms race, there will be no substantial disarmament. If they *both* come to see the futility and danger of it all, they will have come to agree on something that could in itself draw them together and cause them to start unwinding the arms race. But the turnround will require major changes in thinking and in the balance of political forces within both nations.

The disarmament policy and the military policy I am proposing would fit together. They would amount to a policy of rejecting nuclear weapons, starting at home where Britain has power to act.

The Objections

There are five principal objections that are raised against a policy of this kind.

First, it is argued that the United States would quit NATO and go isolationist. I find this highly implausible, though I am ready to believe that it is an argument which fearful people believe and propound with the object of discouraging the adoption of a policy of the kind I am suggesting. The Americans have built up huge investments in production, trading and banking in Europe. Their drive to stop the expansion of Soviet communism, wherever they perceive it, rightly or wrongly, to be a threat, is undiminished. They did not quit Europe when France acted along lines similar to those proposed here.

The notion that Britain alone by changing its policy can persuade the United States to embrace or abandon Europe seems to me an instance of the British disease of post-imperial self-importance.

Secondly, there are those who concede that the Soviet Union is on the defensive and has neither the interest nor the intention to invade Western Europe, but go on to argue that there is a risk that wars might break out in Europe for other reasons, if the present dominance of the Soviet Union and United States over Europe was diminished and their nuclear weapons were removed. The possible causes of those wars that have been mentioned most frequently have been turbulence in Yugoslavia after the death of Tito, popular uprisings in Poland, and an outburst of internal disputes in the Balkans. Most of these things have now happened. Tito has died; at the time of writing, Poland is grappling with popular demands for reform; Greece and Turkey have been quarrelling for a long time. But war has not broken out, and it is hard to see what the *nuclear* confrontation in Europe, as distinct from the alliances and their conventional forces, has contributed to that outcome.

Thirdly, there is the bogey of 'Finlandization'. The story is that if Britain renounces its nuclear weapons, removes American bases, leaves NATO or does almost anything else contrary to military orthodoxy it will be Finlandized, meaning the Soviets will bully us and restrict our liberties as, by implication, they do those of Finland. In fact, Finland enjoys a Western way of life, subject to observing a number of constraints which reassure the Soviets that Finland will not turn hostile or align itself against them.[5] Anyway, why not speak of Swedenization, Austrianization, Yugoslavization, Irelandization or Switzerlandization? Finland is a very special case. It fought against the Soviet Union, but unlike Estonia and Lithuania, it was not absorbed by the Soviet Union – a reminder that the Soviet Union was not indiscriminately expansionist even in 1945.

Fourthly, there is the argument that the nuclear weapons of the Soviet Union and United States and the arms race have kept the peace in Europe since 1945; therefore it is best to go on as we are, hoping they will behave wisely as they keep racing with each other.

The trouble with this argument is that even if it were true that nuclear weapons had prevented war in Europe at some stage since 1945 – which it is impossible to prove – there would be no grounds for saying that they will continue to do so for the lives of our children and grandchildren. The balance of risks changes and must constantly be re-appraised. It is necessary to set out your values and your assessment of the risks and consequences of alternative policies anew, along the lines set out in Part I. To say that we must go on with the policies of the earlier post-war years is to imply that Soviet intentions, the risks of the nuclear arms race and all the other considerations that must be taken into account are the same now as they were then. It is the most mindless form of conservatism with a small 'c'.

Finally, there are two arguments against change as such. One

132

such argument is that change would be dangerous because the system is 'fragile'. That sounds impressive, but the notion that a fragile system necessarily requires inflexible policies, rather than flexible ones, is not sustainable. And it is questionable whether the European system is fragile, except in the sense that there is a dangerous superfluity of nuclear arms which needs to be reduced: the frontier between the two alliances is now well-defined and has remained undisturbed despite various upheavals on either side: for example, uprisings in the Soviet colonies, conflict between Greece and Turkey, the removal of American bases from France, and the diversion of the Americans' attention to Vietnam. The other argument is that for Britain to renounce nuclear weapons would be a sign of weakness and would be humiliating *vis-à-vis* the French. But that is just another version of the argument that nuclear weapons have brought Britain influence or status in the world, an argument dealt with above.

Those who object to a change in policy of the kind suggested here never seem to offer an alternative other than to go on clinging to the United States as it races with the Soviet Union, pleading with it to negotiate agreements on arms control or partial disarmament. They may accept that Britain should give up its own nuclear weapons, or at least refrain from pouring resources into Trident, resources which might otherwise be spent on our conventional forces. That is as far as they will go. They never look far ahead. They think only of the next step in the arms race, the next type of weapon to be acquired by both sides. They do not suggest how the arms race can be ended before it ends us. And that is not surprising. The military, the aerospace and electronics industries, the strategic analysts, the military correspondents all owe their living wholly or largely to the arms race. If they were to question where the arms race is leading us they would be questioning their *raison d'être*. Some of the military, a distinguished few, have spoken up, usually after retirement from the top of the services, and so have a remarkable number of the top scientific advisers who have been drawn into advising governments on nuclear weapons in the United States and Britain, for example Professors Kistiakowsky, Wiesner and York in the United States, and Lord Zuckerman in Britain.[6] Their voices have not yet been heeded.

Conclusion

When asked in an opinion poll in Britain in September 1980 if they expected nuclear war in their lifetime, 48 per cent of the people questioned said yes. Amongst women and the young (aged 15 to 24) the proportion was higher: 55 per cent and 58 per cent.[7]

When half the population expect an event that could mean the end of civilization, the ways of avoiding that event should be the supreme topic of political discussion. Present policies and slogans should be questioned and a search made, starting from first principles, for a way out. That should be an exercise that cuts across political parties and other political issues. In every party, or part of a party, people should be equally concerned to find a better policy; they should be ready to engage with anyone, whatever his politics, in the search for that policy.

In this book I have suggested a framework of analysis and outlined the policy to which I have been led. It is a policy which evolved and changed as I wrote the book. I put it forward as an offering. My aim is to provoke discussion, not conclude it.

Appendix A

**Soviet Motives – Extract from 'Statement on the Defence
Estimates 1980' Volume I, HMSO, 1980**

107. Why has the Soviet Union channelled so much of its national
wealth into the military field, especially over the last decade
when both East and West have been pursuing detente? Several
explanations are possible. First, Soviet leaders regard military
power as a key element in the pursuit of their national aims, and
as the main symbol of their status as a superpower. Second,
Russian thinking has historically favoured large military forces. It
can be argued that experience in World War II moves the Soviet
Union to take out reinforced insurance on defence and that there
is a traditional fear of encirclement, heightened by relative
isolation, past and present, from the rest of the world.

108. There is also an explicitly aggressive motive for the Soviet
military build-up. It is a basic, if nowadays seldom stated, tenet
of Marxist-Leninist philosophy that Communism will ultimately
be extended to every nation and that its spread should be
promoted, if necessary, by military means when the circumstances are right. The Soviet Union has already demonstrated
that it will use force to maintain the Soviet brand of Communism
in Eastern Europe. The invasion of Afghanistan at the end of
1979 was the first example of military intervention to ensure a
Soviet hold on a country outside the Warsaw Pact. The Soviet
Union will, we believe, continue to watch for opportunities to
build up its influence in further countries and will be ready again
to use force. The objective of this drive for influence is to limit
and reduce first the influence and then the security of the West.

109. These are possible explanations or rationalisations for
Soviet military growth. But whatever motives we might ascribe to
Soviet leaders or they themselves might offer as justification, the
Soviet forces facing NATO are very much larger than would, in

our judgment, be needed for defence alone. This is all the more striking in view of the fact that no NATO nation has any aggressive intentions against the Soviet Union, as is reflected in the Alliance's military posture. Moreover, Soviet military doctrine stresses the value of attack with concentrated use of massive force, of achieving strategic surprise by pre-emptive strike and of gaining decisive victories. Soviet forces are organised and trained accordingly. Claims that these forces, despite their massive offensive potential, serve purely defensive purposes can do nothing to reassure the Western nations. NATO must therefore ensure that the Soviet Union could never expect safely to use these forces to defeat NATO in a direct military encounter or to influence Western domestic or international policies. To prevent the Soviet military build-up from diminishing the freedom of action of the Western democracies, there is no alternative but to enhance NATO'S defensive forces to ensure that deterrence is maintained.

110. Soviet strategists hold that any war in Europe is likely to escalate into a nuclear exchange, although they do now seem to accept that a campaign against NATO might start with conventional warfare. Certainly the Soviet leaders have at their disposal the forces to conduct almost any form of campaign that they may regard as necessary. Moreover, their ability to prepare rapidly for war and to launch an attack at a time and place of their own choosing has improved and is still improving. The amount of warning time NATO might receive before attack could be very limited.

111. We have no reason to believe that the present Soviet leaders are deliberately planning to attack NATO. Any such adventurism would be foolhardy in the face of NATO's defences. But, should war ever break out, they intend to win and meanwhile they can use Soviet military power to impress, influence or threaten less powerful nations to adopt policies which suit the Soviet Union. Should NATO lower its guard or falter in its determination to defend itself, the opportunities might prove too tempting. As long therefore as the Soviet Union and its allies sustain and strengthen their large military forces with a pronounced offensive capability, we in the West must continue to ensure that our defences are such that the Warsaw Pact could never count on profiting from the use of military power.

Appendix B

The Military-Industrial Complex: Extract from President Eisenhower's speech delivered on 17 January, 1961 by television and radio.

A vital element in keeping the peace is our military establishment. Our arms must be mighty, ready for instant action, so that no potential aggressor may be tempted to risk his own destruction.

Our military organization today bears little relation to that known by any of my predecessors in peacetime, or indeed by the fighting men of World War II or Korea.

Until the latest of our world conflicts, the United States had no armaments industry. American makers of plowshares could, with time and as required, make swords as well. But now we can no longer risk emergency improvisation of national defense; we have been compelled to create a permanent armaments industry of vast proportions. Added to this, 3½ million men and women are directly engaged in the defense establishment. We annually spend on military security more than the net income of all United States corporations.

This conjunction of an immense military establishment and a large arms industry is new in the American experience. The total influence – economic, political, even spiritual – is felt in every city, every statehouse, every office of the Federal government. We recognize the imperative need for this development. Yet we must not fail to comprehend its grave implications. Our toil, resources, and livelihood are all involved; so is the very structure of our society.

In the councils of government we must guard against the acquisition of unwarranted influence, whether sought or unsought, by the military-industrial complex. The potential for the disastrous rise of misplaced power exists and will persist.

We must never let the weight of this combination endanger our liberties or democratic processes. We should take nothing for granted. Only an alert and knowledgeable citizenry can compel the proper meshing of the huge industrial and military machinery of defense with our peaceful methods and goals so that security and liberty may prosper together.

Source: Public Papers of the Presidents 1960-61, pp. 1037-8, United States Government Printing Office.

Notes to the text

CHAPTER 2

1 *Defence in the 1980s. Statement on the Defence Estimates 1980,* Vol. I, Cmnd.7826-I, London, HMSO, April 1980
2 *Ibid.,* para 111
3 *Ibid.,* paras 120-127
4 *Ibid.,* para 203
5 *Ibid.,* para 130
6 *Ibid.,* para 135
7 Earl Mountbatten of Burma speaking in Strasbourg on 11 May 1979, on the occasion of the award of the Louise Weiss Foundation Prize to Stockholm International Peace Research Institute (SIPRI), of whose Scientific Council he was a member
8 *Afghanistan: the Soviet invasion and its consequences for British policy. Fifth Report from the Foreign Affairs Committee,* House of Commons, 1979-80, p.ix
9 For an excellent brief analysis, see David Holloway, 'War, Militarism and the Soviet State', *Protest and Survive,* ed. E.P. Thompson and Dan Smith, Penguin Special, 1980
10 Lord Carver, *Hansard, House of Lords,* 18 December, 1979, col.1630
11 See also Thomas C. Schelling, 'Nuclear Strategy in Europe', *World Politics,* April 1962, reproduced in *Survival,* International Institute for Strategic Studies (IISS, formerly ISS), London, September October, 1962
12 See Mary Kaldor, *The Baroque Arsenal,* Deutsch (forthcoming)
13 See, for example, *New Conventional Weapons and East-West Security, Parts I and II, Adelphi Papers* 144 and 145, IISS, London 1978 and *Beyond Nuclear Deterrence – New Aims, New Arms,* ed. J. J. Holst and U. Nerlich, Crane, Russak and Co. Inc., New York, and Macdonald and Jane's, London, 1977
14 *SIPRI Yearbook of World Armaments and Disarmament,* (SIPRI Yearbook) 1977, MIT Press and Almquist and Wiksell, Stockholm, 1977, pp 52-82

CHAPTER 3

1 *Armaments and Disarmament in the Nuclear Age, A Handbook,* SIPRI, MIT Press and Almquist and Wiksell, 1976, pp. 62-3
2 See Ralph E.Lapp, *The Weapons Culture,* W. W. Norton, New York, 1968, p.131
3 For a full history of how the missile gap came about within the

intelligence community, see Lawrence Freedman, *U.S. Intelligence and the Soviet Strategic Threat,* Macmillan, 1977

4 See Senator S. Symington, *The Reporter,* 15 February 1962
5 *Public Papers of the Presidents of the United States, John F. Kennedy, 1961,* United States Government Printing Office, 1962, p.68
6 *Ibid.* p.68 and p.153
7 *Ibid.* p.232
8 Robert S. McNamara, *The Essence of Security – Reflections in Office,* Hodder and Stoughton, pp. 57, 58
9 M. Leitenberg, 'Background information on tactical nuclear weapons', in *Tactical Nuclear Weapons: European Perspectives,* SIPRI symposium, ed. F. Barnaby, Taylor and Francis, London, 1978, p.17
10 *Ibid.,* p.7
11 *Ibid.,* p.73
12 For an excellent exposition of the calculus of nuclear destruction in words and algebra see K. Tsipis, *Offensive Missiles,* Stockholm Paper No.5, SIPRI, Stockholm, 1974
13 SIPRI Yearbook 1980, Taylor and Francis, London, p.239
14 Yvon Bourges, French Minister of Defence, cited in D. Bruce Marshall, The Evolving French Strategic Debate, *Strategic Review,* Spring, 1980
15 *The Times,* 12 August, 1980
16 See SIPRI Handbook, *op.cit.,* p.15

CHAPTER 4
1 *Encyclopaedia Britannica*
2 *Nuclear, biological and chemical protection,* Document 838, Assembly of the Western European Union, 29th April, 1980, (hereafter 'WEU Report') para 2.12.
3 *Ibid.* para 2.27
4 *Ibid.* para 2.31
5 *The Times,* 23 September 1980
6 *Worldwide Effects of Nuclear War – Some Perspectives,* United States Arms Control and Disarmament Agency (ACDA) Publication 81, p.5
7 WEU Report para. 2.33
8 ACDA Publication 81, *op.cit.* p.5
9 Naomi Shohno, Kenji Takeshita and Shunzo Okajima, 'Physical Destruction and Human Casualties caused by the Atomic Bombs, Working Document 1, in *A Call from Hibakusha of Hiroshima and Nagasaki,* Proceedings of the International Symposium on the Damage and After-Effects of the Atomic Bombings of Hiroshima and Nagasaki, Pergamon Press, 1978, p.80
10 *The Effects of Nuclear Weapons,* ed Samuel Glasstone and Philip J. Dolan, US Dept. of Defense and US Dept. of Energy, Third Edition 1977, p.545

11 *Ibid.* p.37
12 *Ibid.* pp 300-304
13 Glasstone, 1964 edition, p.350
14 Harold R. Hemingway, The Interactive Dynamics of Nuclear Destruction, *Stanford Journal of International Studies,* Vol.7, 1972, pp. 180-181
15 Glasstone and Dolan, *op.cit.* pp 303-304
16 Hemingway, *op. cit.,* pp.175-6
17 *The Times,* 7 August, 1980
18 Glasstone and Dolan, *op.cit.,* p.545
19 *The Effects of Nuclear War,* US Arms Control and Disarmament Agency (ACDA) April 1979, p.16
20 *Ibid* pp. 16, 23
21 *Ibid* p.26
22 Herman Kahn, *On Thermonuclear War,* Princeton U.P., 1960
23 See in particular Philip Green, *Deadly Logic: The Theory of Nuclear Deterrence,* Ohio State U.P., 1966
24 Herman Kahn, *On Escalation,* Pall Mall Press, London, 1965, p.180. The criticism is made, by Green, *op.cit.,* p.76
25 *The Effects of Nuclear War,* Office of Technology Assessment, Congress of the United States, Croom Helm, London, 1980
26 Roger Beaumont, 'Nuclear Warfare – The illusion of accurate forecasting', *Futures,* February, 1977, p.53
27 Hemingway, *op.cit.,* pp.181-184
28 *Science,* Vol.207, 28 March, 1980, p.1449
29 Carl Friedrich von Weizsäcker, ed., *Kriegsfolgen und Kriegsverhütung,* Munich, Carl Hauser Verlag, 1971, as summarized in English by Alva Myrdal, *The Game of Disarmament,* Manchester U.P., 1977, p.42
30 Lord Zuckerman, 'Science Advisers and Scientific Advisers', address to the American Philosophical Society in Philadelphia, 8 November, 1979, *Proceedings of the American Philosophical Society,* Vol.124, No.4, August 1980, p.9, also reproduced in *Apocalypse Now?,* pamphlet published by Spokesman for the Atlantic Peace Foundation

CHAPTER 5
1 McGeorge Bundy, quoted in Alva Myrdal, *op. cit.,* p.117
2 *Foreign Affairs,* January 1959, pp. 211-234
3 See David Holloway, 'Military Power and Political Purpose in Soviet Policy', in *U.S. Defense Policy in the 1980s,* special issue of *Daedalus,* Journal of the American Academy of Arts and Sciences, Vol. 109, No. 4, Fall 1980
4 See Mary Kaldor, *op. cit.*

CHAPTER 6
1 Arthur I. Waskow, 'American Military Doctrine', reproduced in *Survival,* May-June, 1962, p.107
2 *Ibid.,* p.108

3 Mr McNamara's speech at Ann Arbor, Michigan, on 16 June, 1962, reproduced in *Survival,* September-October, 1962, p.195
4 'Flexible Strategic Options and Deterrence – Excerpts from the Press Conference of United States Secretary of Defense, James Schlesinger, 10 January, 1974', *Survival,* March-April, 1974, p.89
5 *Public Papers of the Presidents,* Richard Nixon, 1970, p.173
6 *Public Papers of the Presidents,* Richard Nixon, 1971, p.310
7 Schlesinger, *op. cit.,* pp. 89-90
8 Harold Brown, Secretary of Defense, 'Strategic Nuclear Policy', speech at Naval War College, Newport, Rhode Island, 20 August, 1980
9 *International Herald Tribune,* 14-15 June, 1980
10 H. Kissinger, cited in Alva Myrdal, *op. cit.,* p.39
11 *NATO Letter,* January, 1965, p.25
12 Alva Myrdal, 'Europe as hostage of the superpowers?', *Bulletin of the Atomic Scientists,* April, 1980, p.4
13 W.F. van Eekelen, Development of NATO's Nuclear Consultation, *NATO Letter* July/August, 1970, p.2
14 *Ibid.,* p.3
15 *Ibid.,* p.6
16 *Ibid.,* p.3
17 *Ibid.,* p.6

CHAPTER 7
1 The list of measures in this section is based on the *SIPRI Yearbook 1980,* pp. 443 to 478 where there is an extremely useful summary of the state of multilateral arms control agreements and bilateral United States/Soviet arms control agreements
2 See *SIPRI Yearbook* 1972, pp. 433-6
3 *SIPRI Yearbook* 1980, p.447
4 Alva Myrdal, *The Game of Disarmament, op. cit.,* p.107
5 For a more complete history of the Partial Test Ban Treaty by the present author, see *SIPRI Yearbook* 1972, Chapter 11
6 See *Nuclear Test Ban Treaty, Hearings before the Committee on Foreign Relations,* United States Senate, August 12-27, 1963, pp. 978, 979, 980
7 *Ibid.,* p.982
8 See Lawrence Freedman, *Britain and Nuclear Weapons,* Papermac, for the Royal Institute of International Affairs, 1980, p.70
9 Nixon cited in Myrdal, *op. cit.,* p.25
10 *Military Posture and National Power,* Statement of the Chairman, U.S. Joint Chiefs of Staff, Fiscal Year 1980
11 *The Times,* 4 June, 1980
12 See Desmond Ball, 'The MX Basing Decision', *Survival,* March/April, 1980, pp. 58-64.
13 *Ibid.,* and also Herbert Scoville Jnr., 'America's Greatest Construction: Can it work?', *New York Review of Books,* 20 March 1980, pp. 12-17

14 Alva Myrdal, *op. cit.*

15 *The Times,* 8 September, 1980

CHAPTER 8

1 Text in Margaret Gowing, *Britain and Atomic Energy, 1939-45,* Macmillan, 1964, pp. 394-436

2 *Ibid.,* pp. 439-40

3 *Ibid.,* p.447

4 See Winston Churchill, *The Second World War,* Vol.VI, Cassell, p.553

5 Margaret Gowing, *Independence and Deterrence – Britain and Atomic Energy 1945-1952,* Macmillan, 1974, Vol.I, p.184

6 *Ibid.,* p.185

7 *Ibid.,* p.212

8 Lawrence Freedman, *Britain and Nuclear Weapons, op. cit.,* p.7

9 *Ibid.,* pp.41-42

10 *Ibid.,* p.55, and *Hansard, House of Commons,* 24 January 1980, col. 681-2

11 See T. A. Stansell Jnr., 'The Many Faces of Transit', *Navigation, Journal of the Institute of Navigation,* USA, Vol.25, No.1, Spring 1978, p.55

12 See Lt Cdr T. R. Lee RN 'Submarine Navigation' *Journal of the Institute of Navigation,* Vol.21, No.4, 1968; Cdr R. G. Haines, 'Eyes and ears on the nuclear patrol', *New Scientist,* August 28, 1969

13 Freedman, *Britain and Nuclear Weapons, op. cit.,* pp.17 and 25

14 *Ibid.,* pp. 17-18

15 *Hansard, House of Lords,* 18 December, 1979, col.1630

16 Freedman, *Britain and Nuclear Weapons, op. cit.,* p.140

17 *Ibid.,* pp. 140-141

18 Gowing, *Independence and Deterrence, op. cit.,* Vol I, pp.158-9

19 Mr Francis Pym, Secretary of State for Defence, *Hansard, House of Commons,* 24 January 1980, col.676

20 *Ibid.,* col. 677

21 *Ibid.,* col. 776

22 Gowing, *Independence and Deterrence, op. cit.,* Vol.I, p.76

23 *Ibid.,* p.250

24 *Ibid.,* pp. 250-1

25 *Ibid.,* p.309

26 *Ibid.,* pp.310 and 310 fn

27 *Ibid.,* p.311

28 S. J. Bond, 'US Third Air Force – A Short History', *Air Britain Digest,* January/February, 1975, p.3

29 Gowing, *Independence and Deterrence, op. cit.,* Vol I, p.312

30 *Ibid.,* p.312

31 *Ibid.,* p.318

32 *Hansard, House of Commons,* 6 December 1951, col.280

33 Gowing, *Independence and Deterrence, op. cit.,* Vol.I, p.413

34 Communiqué jointly issued on January 9, 1952 by Churchill and

Truman after talks at the White House, 7-8 January. *Keesings Contemporary Archive 1952*

35 *Hansard, House of Commons,* 18 June, 1980, col.587; 7 July 1980, col.54 and 8 August 1980, col.481
36 Duncan Campbell, 'Target Britain', *New Statesman,* 31 October 1980, pp. 6-9
37 Gowing, *Independence and Deterrence, op. cit.,* Vol I, p.406
38 Freedman, *Britain and Nuclear Weapons, op. cit.,* p.55
39 Gowing, *Independence and Deterrence, op. cit.,* Vol.I, p.51
40 See Francis Pym, Secretary of State for Defence, *Hansard, House of Commons,* January 24, 1980, col. 672
41 Freedman, *Britain and Nuclear Weapons, op. cit.,* pp. 54-55
42 See Gowing, *Independence and Deterrence, op. cit.,* Vol. I, pp 28-29 and Vol. II, chapter 16
43 See Freedman, *Britain and Nuclear Weapons, op. cit.,* p.52

CHAPTER 9
1 See Harry S. Truman, *Years of Trial and Hope, 1946-1953,* Hodder and Stoughton, 1956, pp.419-420 and p. 435
2 Dwight D. Eisenhower, *Mandate for Change, 1953-56,* Heinemann, 1963, pp.180-181
3 Barry M. Blechman and Stephen S. Kaplan, *Force Without War: US Armed Forces as a Political Instrument,* The Brookings Institution, Washington DC, pp.47-9
4 *Ibid.,* p.49
5 *Nuclear Armament – An Interview with Dr Daniel Ellsberg,* The Conservation Press, Berkeley, California, 1980

CHAPTER 10
1 Lawrence Freedman, *Britain and Nuclear Weapons, op. cit.,* p.140
2 For a description of the French action, including the memoranda addressed by France to its allies, see 'NATO Without France: The Military Implications', Brigadier K. Hunt, *Adelphi Paper Thirty-Two,* ISS, December, 1966
3 I am indebted to Julian Perry Robinson for this point
4 The rules of boxing, named after the ninth marquess of Queensberry, first published in 1867
5 For a good exposition of Finland's position, see Max Jakobson, 'Substance and Appearance: Finland', *Foreign Affairs,* Summer, 1980
6 See Lord Zuckerman, *op. cit.,* esp. pp.14-15
7 Marplan poll conducted for the B.B.C., reported in *The Times,* 22 September, 1980,

INDEX